①

# SELF
# PUBLISHING
## The Essential Guide

Need
— 2 —
Know

D1585495

057525

*Self-Publishing – The Essential Guide* is also available in accessible formats for people with any degree of visual impairment. The large print edition and eBook (with accessibility features enabled) are available from Need2Know. Please let us know if there are any special features you require and we will do our best to accommodate your needs.

First published in Great Britain in 2012 by
Need2Know
Remus House
Coltsfoot Drive
Peterborough
PE2 9JX
Telephone 01733 898103
Fax 01733 313524
www.need2knowbooks.co.uk

# Contents

# Introduction

Self publishing has, historically, had a fairly bad reputation. Many referred to it as 'vanity publishing', there for individuals who wanted to see their name in print, no matter how poor the quality of their writing. Fortunately, the world of book publication has developed massively over the past 5 years and the quality and quantity of books published via a self-publication route has increased significantly. Self-published books can now be found on the bookshelves of Waterstones, Barnes & Noble and even WHSmith. They can be purchased from online shopping stores such as amazon.com, amazon. co.uk and play.com. They can launch the writing careers of up-and-coming writers and can mark the beginning of a new career for the more experienced among us. Importantly, self-published books, and indeed the process of self publishing, has become much more accepted and recognised as a credible way for writers to expose their talent. Self publishing is openly discussed at writing conferences, there is a writing magazine dedicated to this form of publication, and respected writing manuals and reference books such as *The Writers' and Artists' Yearbook* include articles on the subject. Self publishing is a real development in the cultural world of writing, and one that should be celebrated and praised.

'Self-published books can now be found on the bookshelves of Waterstones, Barnes & Noble and even WHSmith.'

## The purpose of this book

*Self Publishing: The Essential Guide* is an interactive reference book that helps you self publish your own manuscript in a step-by-step, digestible way. This book is referred to as 'interactive' because it encourages the reader to participate in specific activities throughout each chapter which in a practical way allows the reader to fulfil the tasks that need to be completed in order to achieve a successful book publication. Each chapter contains a mixture of checklists, reflection points, templates and visual aids to guide the reader through each of the different elements of self publishing. At the end of each chapter you'll find a summary of the key points covered within the chapter, which can act as a reference guide for those readers who want to dip in and dip out of the book and can also provide a handy refresh of the content covered. At the end of this book you'll also find a help list, signposting you onto other useful resources that can further enhance your self-publishing journey.

## Who is this book for?

This book has been written to support anyone and everyone who is interested in publishing their own book. It can also act as a handy reference guide for anyone studying the art of book publication, or who has an interest in how self publishing works.

## How will this book help me write my very own novel?

The content contained in this book is split into 9 comprehensive yet accessible chapters. Each chapter contains a number of headings and subheadings to guide you through the content in an easy and logical way. As you work your way through this book you'll find information, instructions and resources to help you complete each aspect of self publishing including:

- Learning what makes a good self-published book.
- Preparing your manuscript for publication.
- Proofreading, editing and typesetting.
- Printing your book.
- Understanding the importance of paper quality, ink quality and a good bind!
- Marketing your book.
- Throwing a launch party.
- Negotiating with book stores and distributers.
- Managing royalties.

Overall, it is hoped that this guide will provide you with the confidence and motivation you need to fulfil your dream of publishing your very own book and seeing your ideas and concepts printed on paper – there for you to share with the world.

# Chapter One
## Why Self Publish?

So, you've finally finished writing that book that you've been thinking about, planning and drafting for some time now and you're wondering what steps to take next. Perhaps the biggest decision you need to make is focused on the publication route of the book. Are you going to approach traditional publishers or literary agents in a bid to secure a publishing contract? Or do you fancy leading the publication of the book yourself, by following a self-publishing path?

Self publishing is a route taken by an ever increasing number of authors. Nowadays many writers, some well established, others novices, find that choosing to self publish their work simply adds to the pleasure they gain from writing. After all, as a self-published author you find that you have full control over the way in which the words that you have lovingly drafted are finalised, printed and sold to the general public. This in turn can mean that your career as an author is actually more successful as you are able to control your public appearances, take a larger cut of the royalty payments, and determine when, where and how your book is marketed. Self publishing your work is, however, a task that requires a large amount of time, enthusiasm and commitment. It is therefore important to be sure that the route of self publishing is right for you, before you start to embark upon it.

'Self publishing is a route taken by an ever increasing number of authors.'

## Self publishing: the pros

There are so many positive reasons for choosing to self publish a manuscript rather than deciding to go down the more traditional route of seeking a publishing company or a literary agent to take on the publication of your work. Some of the more common, positive reasons for choosing a self publishing approach include:

- Content control. When an author signs themselves up with a traditional publishing house, they are likely to find that the publishing company has the final say on book content. This can mean that the author is forced to make or accept changes to the content of the book they've written, whether they agree with the changes made or not. This can lead to a great deal of frustration and anger. By self publishing your book this potential problem area is resolved as the author remains in control of the book content at all times.

- Creative control. As an author you are likely to have strong views on the way in which your book is presented to the general public as a finished item. You may, for example, feel strongly about the book cover that is provided, the paper that the book is printed on to, the quality of any internal illustrations, graphics or photographs, the format and size of the book and even the place-marking ribbons. Whilst a traditional publishing company may welcome your suggestions over these specifications, they won't necessarily take all of your ideas on board. As a self publisher, you can work closely with a printer to ensure that the vision you hold of your book is turned into a reality.

- Time. Self publishing a book takes time and commitment. However, seeking a literary agent or a traditional publishing house to take on your work can actually take up an awful lot more of your time than you may first envisage. To stand a chance of securing a publishing contract in this way you will need to first identify agents or publishers who are open to publishing books of the same genre as your own. Then you'll need to pull together a 'publisher pack'; a portfolio of information about you as an author, your work, the marketability of your book, a synopsis of your book and some sample chapters from your book. Finally you'll need to submit these publisher packs to your chosen publishers and agents. It can take months for the replies to come in, and if they are negative, you'll find that you have to start the whole process over again. Self publishing by contrast is a process that you, the author, are in control of. To a large extent you can therefore determine the speed at which actions take place, and thus you are able to dictate how quickly your work is transformed from drafted manuscript to printed books that are for sale in local book stores and via online distribution sites.

- Financial gains. The majority of traditional publishers offer a low rate of royalties to authors. When a book that has been published by a traditional publisher is sold, the average royalty percentage for the author is 10%. However, a book that has been self published can leave the author with a royalty figure of between 40% and 60% of the book price.

- Marketing management. Self publishing allows you the freedom to market your book in a way that excites you and in a way that fits in with your work and personal commitments. It may be that the publication of this book is your principle focus. That's great and is likely to mean that you have a greater level of flexibility in terms of time availability. However, for an author who is trying to manage the publication of their book alongside leading family life and holding down a full-time job, free time to dedicate to marketing their book may be a rarity. In either case, the beauty of self publishing is that it enables you to do as much or as little promotional activity for your book as required. It may be that you want to throw a launch party to celebrate the release of your book. Or you may simply want to circulate a couple of press releases about the book across your local community. Self publishing allows you to do either, or both.

## Self publishing: the cons

Self publishing does, however, have a downside and there are a number of negatives or 'obstacles' that need to be thought through when considering a self-publication route. The key areas for consideration are:

- Isolation. Working with a traditional publishing house brings with it the security of a full team of skilled individuals who are committed to investing their time and talents into your book. The pool of skills needed to create a book is quite remarkable; editors, proofreaders, those involved in page layout, printers, marketers, designers, distributers, accountants . . . the list is endless. As a self publisher, it is down to the individual author to either fulfil all of these roles themselves or to source external expertise. The prospect of doing either can be daunting and authors can often feel lonely and stressed by the need to project manage the creation of their book independently.

'Self publishing allows you the freedom to market your book in a way that excites you and in a way that fits in with your work and personal commitments.'

- Time. Self publishing may in many ways be less time-consuming than seeking a traditional publishing deal, but nonetheless it is still a task that requires a large amount of personal time commitment. And time, as we all know, is precious.

- Financial investment. When it comes to self publishing you have to spend a little to gain a little. Self publishing your book comes with a price tag; it will need to be proofread, it will need a cover design, a printer, an ISBN number, and some form of marketing. All of these requirements cost money, and whilst there is the potential to gain back this investment through royalties made on book sales, it may take some time to recoup the costs initially laid out.

- Prestige. If your self-published book has an amateurish look and feel about it then readers may think less of it in terms of its literary value. It is therefore important to plan your self publication carefully, and to ensure that important issues such as paper quality, print resolution and proofreading have all been built into your plan.

'When it comes to self publishing you have to spend a little to gain a little.'

## Is self publishing the best route for you?

So, now that you've had an opportunity to consider the positives and negatives of self publishing a book, it is time to determine if self publishing really is the best publishing route for you!

The table opposite lists a number of questions about your motivation for publishing your book, your access to resources that will support the publication of your book and your personal time management and organisational skills. Work through each of the questions in the table and choose the response that best meets your own personal viewpoint or circumstance.

| Question | Response A | Response B | Response C |
|---|---|---|---|
| Why did you decide to write your book? | I believe I have the talent to become a successful writer | I had a great idea for a book and I just had to write it down | I have a desire to see my name in print |
| What do you think makes a book successful? | The number of copies it has sold | If the writer is happy with the end product | If it provides new information for the world to consider or enjoy |
| What would make you feel as if your book was a success? | I am receiving an income from the book | The book is completed | The book is available for purchase from a number of bookstores |
| How important to you is it that you are considered by others to be a successful author? | Very important | Quite important | Unimportant |
| On a scale of 1-10, where does the publication of your book rate in terms of importance? | Between 8 and 10 | Between 3 and 5 | Between 5 and 8 |
| Would it matter to you if another person dictated the content, style and look of your published book? | Not particularly | Yes a little | Yes |
| How much time do you have to dedicate to the marketing of your book? | A small amount of free time | Quite a lot | As much as is needed |
| Are you daunted by the prospect of managing the publication of your book? | Yes | Yes, but I would be happy to enlist the support of others | I see it as an enjoyable challenge |
| Are you an organised person? | I can be if needed | Yes I am very organised and 'list' orientated | I can be if the task in hand is important to me |
| Do you believe that self-published books are in some way less worthy than those published by a traditional publisher? | Yes | They don't have to be, if they are well created and printed | No |

Individuals who felt that Response B and/or Response C best matched their own viewpoint will find that self publishing would be a perfect publication route forward for their book(s). However, if you found that the responses listed in the column titled 'Response A' best matched your own viewpoint then you may want to reconsider following the self publication route. Take some time to explore or re-explore following a traditional publication path before committing yourself to the journey of self publication.

## Advice from others who have successfully self published

It takes courage, passion, enthusiasm and dedication to self publish, and as we have seen above, the journey to successful self publication can at times be a lonely one. Ultimately however, to see your book in print, to hold it in your hands and to walk past a shop window and see it on display is such a wonderful feeling – it is well worth the effort! Below, a number of self-published authors have provided their own snippets of advice on the self-publishing process. Take what you can from this, as advice from others who have walked the same path as you is always invaluable.

'It takes courage, passion, enthusiasm and dedication to self publish.'

*'Quality is hugely important when it comes to creating a self-published book. There still exists a stereotype of self-published books – that they are poor or amateurish in quality. Don't allow your book to fall into this category. Enlist the expertise of proofreaders, of cover designers and of printers to ensure that your book reads and looks as good as it possibly can.'* Samantha Pearce, author of *Tangled Heaven*.

*'1 – Don't risk more money than you can afford. 2 – As a rule, it is not advisable to price your book much lower than the going rate for the kind of book it is; a lower price means a lower profit for booksellers and reduces their incentive to order. 3 – Take all the advice you can get from anyone who knows what they are talking about.'* Jill Paton Walsh and John Rowe Townsend.

*'You need to be organised when publishing your own book. Draw up a timetable of tasks that need to be completed to ensure the smooth publication of your book. Work backwards from the date that you want your book to be available for purchase. And always allow slippage time . . . because you will most definitely need it!* Catherina Dunphy, successful self-publishing ghost writer.

# Examples of good self-published books

It can be a huge help to take a look at the written work of other self-published authors in order to identify what a strong self-published book looks like, and to gather ideas for the final creation of your own book. Listed below are the names of ten authors and the titles of their self-published books. You can use this list as a starting point, before going on to review self-published books that match the genre or style of your own book title.

*Thermogenesis* by Sally-Ann Voak.

*Gothique Fantastique* by Ron Clooney.

*Phoenix in a Bottle* by Lilian and Murdoch MacDonald.

*Eric and the Wooly Jumpers* by Malcolm Hulme.

*African Nights* by Linda Louisa Dell.

*Dear Dylan* by Siobhan Curham.

*Mirabelle the Lost Kitten* by Sarah Gaichies.

*More than Words* by Marrilynne Taylor.

*Catherina and the Incredible Stripy Pants* by Samantha Pearce.

*The Xandra Function* by Alan Cash.

*Unravelling* by Lindsay Stanberry-Flynn.

# Summing Up

- Before embarking upon a self-publishing journey, it is important to consider each of the pros and cons associated with self publishing in order to be absolutely sure that this is the best publishing approach for you and for your writing.

- There are many positives attached to self publishing including: control over the content, technical specifications and design of your book, better royalty profits, control over the advertising and marketing of your book, and a short time frame in terms of book production.

- There are also associated negatives to the self publishing process that should be considered. These include isolation, a need to invest financially in the publication of your book, and a huge reliance on your own time, enthusiasm and dedication.

- Think about the motivation that sits behind your desire to see your book published, seek advice from other self-published authors and take a look at some previously self-published titles before deciding if the self-publishing route is right for you.

# Chapter Two

# The Different Routes to Self Publication

So, you've decided to self publish your manuscript, your collection of poetry or your set of short stories. You now need to think about *how* you are going to publish your work. Are you going to enlist the support of a self-publishing company; using their expertise to direct the creation of your book, or are you going to take on full responsibility for the production of your book – from typesetting, to cover design, to final print and distribution? Let's look at what is involved in either case.

## Enlisting the support of a self-publishing company

There are a number of publishing houses out there that work with self-published authors. Sometimes these publishing houses also work with authors who are being published in a traditional way, i.e. the publishing house has commissioned the author's work. Other publishing houses are solely in place to work with self-publishing authors. In either case, it is likely that the service you will be offered as a self-publishing author will broadly be the same. Self-publishing companies are there to effectively 'build' your book for you. With this in mind, they should be able to provide you with the following services:

※ An editor (or a list of recommended editors).

※ A proofreader (or a list of recommended proofreaders).

※ A book designer.

※ A cover designer or artist.

'You now need to think about *how* you are going to publish your work.'

- An ISBN number.

- A printer.

- A range of distribution options/contracts.

- Marketing support.

What's more, self-publishing companies should be able to tailor their services to meet your specific requirements. After all, most (if not all) self-publishing companies use the same technologies to produce books, and offer a similar mix of services. It is the flexibility in their service provision, the publishing house's approachability and client relationship ethos, and the amount of choice they provide to authors, which marks out the differences between each of the companies. These are the areas you will want to focus upon when deciding which self-publishing company to choose. Don't forget, you as the author will be paying the self-publishing company for their role in the creation of your book. As a paying customer, you will want to ensure that you are provided with the service that you desire, at as competitive a rate as possible.

'Use a resource such as *The Writers' and Artists' Yearbook* or an Internet search which includes the key words "self-publishing company" to identify a long list of self-publishing agents.'

## Creating a shortlist

There are quite literally hundreds of companies that now offer publishing services to self-publishing authors. That's quite a list to work through! In order to identify a publishing house that will best meet your requirements, you first need to pull together a shortlist of self-publishing companies from which to choose from. Use a resource such as *The Writers' and Artists' Yearbook* (see the help list) or an Internet search which includes the key words 'self-publishing company' to identify a long list of self-publishing agents. From this long list, aim to create a shortlist that contains no more than 10 companies. Use the following criteria to shorten your long list appropriately:

- Cost. What budget do you have to spend on the creation of your book? Exclude marketing costs from this budget. Remove any companies from your list where their prices (or indicative prices) exceed your budget.

- Location. Some authors feel happier working with a publishing company that is physically located close to their home town. If this is true for you, remove any companies that are situated too far away from where you live.

- Testimonials. Is there any evidence that previous customers have been unsatisfied with the work produced by the self-publishing company? If so, remove this company from your list. You don't want to run the risk of disappointment when your books are finally produced.

- Breadth of service. Does the self-publishing company offer you everything you need to produce your book? Will they support with ISBN registration? Provide a cover design? Liaise with distributors on your behalf? If they can't provide all of the service elements you need, exclude them from the list.

- General feel. Sometimes you just feel as if a company won't work for you. That's fine and often your intuition is right. Remove any companies that you're just not sure of; even if you don't know what is causing your uncertainty.

## Questions to ask

Now that your shortlist has been finalised, the next step is to identify the self-publishing company that you are ultimately going to work with. This is the time to focus on the specifics of their service delivery and on the flexibility of their service provision. The table overleaf contains information on a set of key questions that you can pose to your shortlisted self-publishing companies, in order to identify your preferred publishing body.

More information on what you can expect from a self-publishing company can be found in chapter 5 – Using a Self-Publishing Company.

# Signing a contract

Once you have identified a self-publishing company to work with and have run through your specifications with them, you are likely to be asked to sign a copy of their writer's contract before work on the production of your book can begin. Such a contract is there to protect both parties; you (the author) will want written confirmation that your books will be produced in line with your expectations, and the publishing company will want written confirmation that their fees will be paid as required.

'An ISBN is an International Standard Book Number – it is the number used by booksellers and distributors to identify and order copies of books.'

| Question | Key points surrounding this question |
|---|---|
| Will I own the text and supporting files used to print my book? Will they be supplied to me at the end of the production process? | Self publishing by default should mean that you personally retain all rights to your book. It is therefore imperative that you check that you will own every single piece of the book production process, from the copy edited manuscript to the files used to print your book, and if required, you should be able to get hold of these files at any time from the publishing company. |
| Am I able to terminate my contract with you, without penalty, if I so choose? | The contract you have with the self-publishing company should be easy to understand. It shouldn't contain any clause that locks you into keeping your book with that specific self-publishing company, and you shouldn't be penalised if you decide that you no longer want to publish your book with that particular company. |
| Can I set my own retail price for the book? | Having control over the retail price of your book means that it is unlikely to be set too high for the genre market. |
| How much will it cost me to buy copies of my book from you? | The price of purchasing copies of your own book should be fixed; and the rate should offer a significant discount on the retail price. |
| What will my royalty rate be and what is my royalty rate based on? | Royalty rates should be higher for self-published books than those seen on books that are published traditionally. Make sure that this is the case for your book. Also identify what figure the publishing company will use to base your royalty rate on. Is it on the net sale for example, or on the retail price of the book? |
| Will you use a set template for my cover design? | Lots of self-publishing companies have a number of book cover templates that they systematically use to create book covers for their authors, tweaking them slightly for each individual client. You may be happy with this approach, or you may want confirmation that your design will be unique. |
| Will you register my book for an ISBN? | An ISBN is an International Standard Book Number – it is the number used by booksellers and distributors to identify and order copies of books. Your book will need to have its own ISBN before it can be distributed or sold. |
| How will you support me in the sales and distribution of my book? | Some self-publishing companies will list your book for you on websites such as Amazon and Lulu. Others will help you get your book into local bookstores. |

# What does a self-publishing contract look like?

A self-publishing contract shouldn't be complicated. It should be free from legal jargon and should be relatively short in length. The key things that should be contained within a self-publishing contract are:

- The fact that the work produced, and the files used to produce the work, all belong to you, the author.

- Permission from you to the self-publishing company to use your work in order to produce, distribute and sell a book.

- Responsibilities that sit with the author, in terms of how the manuscript needs to be submitted to the publishing company.

- The fact that the publishing company is not liable for lost profits or revenues that are due to, related to or connected with the book.

- The fact that the self-publishing company is not liable for any errors with the book (i.e. typos).

- Information on how royalties will be paid.

- Information on the fees associated with the production of the book, and timescales for the payment of these fees.

## Reading the small print

Self publishing contracts are generally fairly standard and don't run more than 2 to 3 pages of A4. Nonetheless, it is important to read the contract thoroughly to ensure that: (a) you understand each of the points contained within the contract, (b) you are happy with the information contained in the contract, and (c) there isn't anything missing from the contract that you believe should be added. It can also be helpful to have someone else read through the contract too, as they may identify areas of uncertainty that you had initially missed. If you feel that your contract is so complex that you need legal support to understand the contents then be cautious in the way that you precede with the self-publishing company. An over-jargoned contract does raise questions about the reliability of the company itself.

'An over-jargoned contract does raise questions about the reliability of the company itself.'

## Be cautious of what you're signing

If, having read through the contract several times, you feel that there are a number of points within the contract that you'd like clarifying or if you are unhappy with the content of the contract, be sure to raise your queries with the self-publishing company prior to signing. Ensure that you are happy with their response to each of your points before finally signing and returning the contract.

# Going it alone

Of course you don't have to enlist the support of an established publishing house to turn your manuscript into a sellable book. You can take full control of the publishing process and complete each of the tasks involved in self publishing a book single-handedly, calling on the support of specialists as and when you need to. There are a number of positive reasons for working in this way, for example; you retain full control of the book creation – you personally choose the quality of paper that the book is printed on, the graphics for the book jacket, the number of books that are printed at any one time, and the price of the book. In addition, some self-publishing authors feel a strong desire to be able to say that they took full responsibility for the creation of their book, and so don't feel comfortable with using a self-publishing company. Managing the full publication of your book can also be extremely rewarding, and if you plan to write and self-publish further titles, then the relationships you'll have built up with distributors, printers, proofreaders etc. will be vital to the successful delivery of future titles.

## What does 'going it alone' *really* entail?

If you plan to publish your book without enlisting the help of a self-publishing company then you will need to think about the following key areas:

- Book format and cover options.
- Print technology and paper quality.
- Number of pages, page size and margins.
- Book binding.
- Formatting of content, including font types, colours and sizes, line spacing, indentation, and page numbers.

- Copy editing and proofreading.
- The price of the book.
- ISBN registration.
- Book distribution.
- Marketing and advertising.

The table below looks at the key issues you need to consider against each of the areas listed above. Chapter 6 – Going It Alone, then looks at some of these crucial issues in greater detail.

| Publishing area | Associated issues/points for consideration |
|---|---|
| Book format and cover options | Think about whether or not you'll want to publish your book in hardback. Hardback books are becoming less and less popular; however they do offer the ability to charge a higher price for each copy of the book, and the costs associated with printing a hardback book aren't significantly higher than those associated with printing a paperback.<br><br>A self-published book needs to be produced to the same quality standard as that seen in a book produced by a traditional publishing house. The quality of the cover design is therefore crucial. If you are not a graphic designer or artist then it is worth enlisting the support of a skilled individual who can create a customised cover design for you. |
| Print technology and paper quality | The two principle print technologies used to produce books are digital and lithography. Generally speaking, digital printing is more cost-effective if you are looking to produce between 300 and 500 copies of your book; for print runs larger than 500, lithography is often a more cost-effective approach. Lithography also tends to reproduce photos and other coloured images in finer detail; so if your book contains a lot of imagery then lithography might just be the best option for you. The best way to choose between the two print options is to ask a printer to produce a couple of pages of your book using the two different print technologies. Then decide from there.<br><br>It is always a good idea to discuss the paper type on which your book will be printed with your chosen printer. The majority of paperbacks produced are printed on paper that is 80gsm (grams per square metre). You could however choose paper that is anything up to 170gsm. The higher the gsm, the thicker the pages, and thus the thicker the book. |

'Hardback books are becoming less and less popular; however they do offer the ability to charge a higher price for each copy.'

| | |
|---|---|
| Number of pages, page sizes and margins | Printers require a book to have an even number of pages, so you may need to think about adding in a blank page or an additional page of text. |
| | Take a look at published books that are the same genre as your own book. What size are the majority of these books? Are you happy for your book to be of a similar size? Ensure that your printer is aware of the page size you require, as this may impact on the number of pages that your drafted text spans. |
| | Margins are important because they help make a page appear attractive to a reader. First check that your printer doesn't have any guidance on print margins. Then take a look at a range of printed books and decide what margin dimensions you prefer. Remember that you'll need a largish margin on the spine side of each page, to accommodate the book binding. |
| Formatting the content | Consistency is important when it comes to formatting your content. Ensure that you are consistent in the way that you use font types, colours and sizes. Furthermore, stick to the same line spacing and depth of paragraph indentation. |
| | Page numbers should be included in all books. If you are using preliminary pages (i.e. any page that sits before the introduction) should have lower case italic Roman numerals (*i, ii, iii, iv*). |
| Copy editing and proofreading | For your book to appear professional to readers, the text will need to be squeaky clean. The best way to guarantee that the text of your book is accurate is to have it professionally proofread – don't be fooled into thinking that you can proofread your own work, or that you can enlist the help of a friend or family member to do this for you. |
| Book price | Pricing your book is important; too high and you won't attract readers. Too low and your profit margin will be minimal. Take a look at the retail price of other books that are of a similar genre and length to your manuscript and use this information to set a realistic price for your book. |
| ISBN registration | Your book will need an ISBN number if you wish to make it available for purchase. ISBN numbers can be purchased from Nielsen (see the help list) in batches of 10. |
| Book distribution | Think about registering your book with large online and offline book distribution companies such as Nielsen, Amazon, Gardners and Bertrams. They all have information on their websites regarding how to register your publication with them (see the help list). |

# Summing Up

▓ When it comes to publishing your book there are two possible approaches; enlisting the support of a self-publishing company or 'going it alone'.

▓ There are pros and cons to each approach; some individuals find it more efficient and less stressful to utilise a self-publishing company, others enjoy the challenge of single-handedly producing their own book.

▓ Regardless of which approach you choose, be sure to focus on the quality of your book production. Cover design, the quality and accuracy of the book content and the registration of your book with key distributors are all crucial to the success of your publication.

'Cover design, the quality and accuracy of the book content and the registration of your book with key distributors are all crucial to the success of your publication.'

# Chapter Three

# Preparing Your Manuscript for Publication

Regardless of whether you choose to publish your manuscript via a self-publishing house or whether you choose to publish your manuscript independently, the first step in producing your finished book is to finalise the book content. This requires editing the text, proofreading the text, typesetting the manuscript and finalising any illustrations that will be included with the book.

## Seeking the views of others

It is important to remember that anyone and everyone who reads your book will form an opinion on the contents of it. By publishing your book, you are putting it out there into the big wide world for an audience to review. Each and every one of us is different and so we'll all have our own opinions, our own likes and our own dislikes. There will be some individuals who will read your book and will instantly connect with the storyline, with the lead characters or with the facts being conveyed. There will be others who are less enthusiastic about the book; and there will be some individuals who choose not to read the book at all – put off by the book genre or perhaps by the cover of the book jacket. It is perfectly natural to find that readers react differently to your publication.

It can, however, be helpful to identify individuals who can read your book ahead of its publication and who can offer you valuable feedback on the contents of the book. This not only gives you an opportunity to reconsider parts of the book based on feedback, but it also prepares you for the fact that there may be some people who just don't get on all that well with your text.

'The first step in producing your finished book is to finalise the book content.'

There are a number of ways that you can intentionally gather feedback on your manuscript before it is finalised for publication:

- Hand your manuscript to a friend or family member to read and comment upon.
- Hand your manuscript to a tutor or mentor to read and comment upon.
- Place your writing on a blog or writing website and welcome comments from others.
- Send your work into a professional editorial or manuscript review company and ask them to provide you with a full report on your work.

There are a number of reasons why writers seek feedback and reviews of their writing. Key reasons include:

- Enabling them to be signposted to areas of weakness within their manuscript, which they can then work upon to improve the entire text.
- To receive constructive criticism.
- To be able to discuss their manuscript intelligently, in order to further build up their own knowledge of the subject area that they have written about.
- To locate encouragement and support.
- To motivate themselves to either look again at the manuscript they have completed, or to commence a new piece of creative writing.
- To build self-esteem.

# Copy editing and proofreading

Once you've received some feedback on your book from trusted friends, family members or colleagues, and you've made any required amendments, the next step is to ensure that your text is copy edited and proofread. All traditional publishing houses will ensure that the work of their authors is copy edited and proofread; as a self-publishing author it is important that you do the same.

## So, what do a copy editor and a proofreader actually do?

A proofreader's role is to ensure accuracy and style consistency of a manuscript. This means correcting errors in spelling, grammar and punctuation. It also includes ensuring that the manuscript is consistent in terms of use of numbers, capitalisations and the hyphenating of words.

A copy editor will look at the style of an author's writing and will make amendments to the text that improves the flow of a particular section of writing. This could include breaking down over-long sentences or rewriting sentences that are confusing to the reader.

It is always best to use the editorial services of a professional company or individual who is qualified and experienced in copy editing and proofreading. You may find a single company or individual who can offer both services, or you may need to enlist the support of two separate individuals or organisations to complete each of the tasks for you. If the latter is the case, have your manuscript copy edited first, and then send it on to your chosen proofreader for a final read through and text correction.

## Copy editing

There are a number of ways to locate a copy editor. The most straight forward way of finding a copy editor that you are happy with is to do an online search for copy editors; narrowing your search according to factors that are important to you. For example, you may want your editor to be located close to where you live or work, or you may want them to have specialist experience and expertise in editing books that fall within the same genre as your own title.

Once you have pulled together a list of copy editors that meet your initial specifications, you'll need to narrow down your search to one specific editorial company or independent copy editor. The checklist overleaf will help you do just that. It contains key areas of expertise that you should go through with each of your shortlisted copy editors, before deciding on the individual or organisation that is right for you.

'A proofreader's role is to ensure accuracy and style consistency of a manuscript.'

## Checklist of copy editor credentials

- Training: What specific copy editing training has the individual completed?

- Qualifications: What relevant qualifications has the individual obtained, and when were the qualifications obtained?

- Experience: How much experience does the copy editor have? How relevant is this experience to your personal requirements?

- Interpersonal and communication skills: How well do you think you'd get on with the copy editor? Do you feel comfortable working with them? Do you believe that he/she would be sensitive in the way that they approached your work and/or raised queries about your work?

- Judgement: How well can the editor make their own decisions about style application? Do they have any positive examples of when they have had to deal with conflicts of interest between themselves and the writer over style application or content amendment?

- Sensitivity: What are their thoughts on making amendments to the text in a way that is in keeping with your own voice and style?

- Adherence to deadline: Are you confident that the deadline you'd be setting would indeed be met?

- Cost: Are you happy with the price quoted and with the way in which this price has been determined?

Once your chosen copy editor has been commissioned, you'll need to fully brief that individual or company on the work that you require them to deliver for you. This is an important stage in the production and development of your book. Get the brief right and you should find that having your manuscript copy edited is a relatively pain-free experience!

It is generally preferable to speak to your allocated copy editor over the phone or in person before they commence work on your book. That way you can have a detailed discussion about your book, about the copy editing process and about your personal expectations. It can be helpful to follow this conversation up in writing, generally by sending the copy editor an email which outlines the key points of the conversation held. By putting down this information on paper, both parties have a clear understanding of the work that needs to be delivered, and the manner in which it is likely to be completed.

On a day-to-day basis, liaison with your copy editor will predominately be via email. You will also need to email over all of the documentation your editor will need to comprehensively complete the copy edit of your manuscript. The table below outlines the type of documentation and information you may need to send to the copy editor.

| | |
|---|---|
| Synopsis | A brief outline of your book will help the copy editor understand the storyline or book structure before he/she commences the edit. |
| The full manuscript | Preferably in a Word document format and either as one full document or separated out into chapters. |
| A list of outstanding material | Is there anything that you are yet to have sent to the editor? If so, provide details of the outstanding documentation and state when the editor can expect to receive this information. |
| Specific instructions | What level of editing do you want your copy editor to undertake? Are you limiting their involvement in the text or are you happy for them to make as many changes as they deem necessary? Are there any other tasks that you are expecting the editor to undertake, such as preparing preliminary pages? |
| Photography and illustrations | If your manuscript contains photos, illustrations or graphics it is important to let the editor know if you require an editorial of the labels attached to these images, and to clarify whether or not images can be re-sized by the editor. |
| Administration | Confirm to the copy editor who it is that they should liaise with regarding any queries they have over the text. It might also be worthwhile to ask the editor to prepare handover notes that can be passed to your chosen proofreader, once the copy edit has been completed. |
| Terms and conditions | Outline formally the terms and conditions associated with this piece of work. This should include the agreed cost of the copy edit, how and when payment is due to be made, what will and won't be reimbursed, and when the completed copy edit should be returned to you. |

'A brief outline of your book will help the copy editor understand the storyline or book structure before he/she commences the edit.'

## Proofreading

Once your manuscript has been through a copy editing process, it is ready to be passed to a proofreader. Locating a proofreader that you are happy with is just as important as determining the most appropriate copy editor for you. Use the previous checklist (in the section titled 'Copy editing' within this chapter) to choose a proofreader or proofreading company that best meets your needs.

Once your proofreader has been determined, you'll need to send through all of the information and documentation that the proofreader needs to complete the desired work. This documentation is likely to be similar to that sent off to your copy editor previously. As before, you'll need to include:

- The full manuscript.

- Details of any missing information.

- Specific instructions regarding how the proofread should be completed, and how the final manuscript should be presented to you.

- The copy editor's handover report (if applicable).

- The terms and conditions of your working arrangement; including information relating to fees, deadlines and presentation format.

## Proofreading your own manuscript

It is always preferable to use a professional and experienced proofreader, as whilst the majority of us think that we can apply the rules of grammar and punctuation relatively easily, it is very difficult to catch your own writing errors because when you read through your own work you tend to read what you *expect* to see as opposed to what has actually been written.

However, if you are an experienced writer or if you find that your budget won't stretch to incorporate the fees associated with a professional proofreader, then there are things that you can do to eliminate as many proofreading errors as possible within your own work. The list opposite provides some helpful tips for proofreading your own work independently:

- Proofreading is easier to do from a printed copy of your text.

- Look out for errors that you frequently make, such as using the word 'you' instead of 'your'.

- Look out for words that are commonly misused, misspelled, or sound similar but have different meanings, such as; except/accept, moral/morale, intense/intensive etc.

- Try to review your manuscript with fresh eyes – don't commence a proofread as soon as you've finished writing the final version of your book.

- If possible, proofread your work twice.

- Most of us use a spell checker program, a software tool that allows writers to check their spelling, when we write on the computer. It is a terrific aid to proofreading, but it does not replace a dictionary and the need to proofread carefully for several reasons. Let's review what a spell checker program can and cannot do.

## Spell check

The spell check feature on most computer Word document programs is a fantastic aid that can be used by proofreaders and writers to help them locate and amend spelling and grammar errors. However, a spell checker cannot act as a substitute for a full manual proofread of your manuscript. For whilst it can help identify misspelled words, the incorrect use of capital letters, and highlight to you when a word has been typed twice in immediate succession, it cannot:

- Find typographical errors that appear to be correct ('form' instead of 'from', 'be long' instead of 'belong') for example.

- Point out grammatical errors ('their' instead of 'they're', 'its' instead of 'it's') for example.

- Identify poor sentence sense and syntax.

'A spell checker cannot act as a substitute for a full manual proofread of your manuscript.'

# Typesetting

In general terms, typesetting refers to the composition of printed text on a page. When it comes to manuscripts, the term typesetting therefore relates to how the written text is arranged on each of the pages of your book. If typesetting has been completed accurately, then the text on each page of your book should be easy on the eye, it should flow seamlessly from one page to another and the reader shouldn't be distracted by the composition of the text on the page; instead they should be drawn into the content of the text instead. The only exception to this is if the composition of the text is deliberately different; in the expression of modern poetry for example.

If you choose to use a self-publishing company to support the publication of your book then you are likely to find that they will automatically typeset your manuscript for you. This will ensure that the margins of each page of the book are consistent, that the line spacing on each page of the book is the same, and that the positioning of the text on each page of the book is appropriate.

If, however, you have taken full control of the book publication, you may find that you need to organise the typesetting of your manuscript yourself. Some printing companies can typeset your manuscript prior to printing copies of your book, and so this is a service option that you can always explore with your chosen printer. Some self-publishing authors, however, choose to typeset their manuscript themselves.

Typesetting independently can be quite a long process, but a methodical one. Each page of your book will need to be examined individually, to ensure that the way in which the text is laid out on paper is consistent and attractive.

By following the steps below, you can create a fully typeset version of your manuscript, which is ready to pass for printing:

- Remove any instances of consecutive spacing after a full stop, semicolon etc., so that there is only one space between each word or punctuation marking.

- Ensure paragraph indentation is consistent throughout.

- Check dashes, ellipses and other typographical elements used within your manuscript to ensure that the spacing before and after each element is consistent.

- Ensure that hyphenated words are not split across two lines.

- Justify the text and ensure that margin sizes are consistent.

- Check that there is more than one word on the last line of each paragraph

- Manipulate the text if necessary to ensure that all pages are of the same length.

- Check each title or chapter heading for awkward character combinations. Do some letters within these words appear too squashed together? If so you may need to manually increase the spacing between these letters.

## Illustrations

In the publishing industry, the term 'illustration' refers to any graphic element, including photographs, graphs, charts, maps and drawings. So anything that you include in your book that isn't text can be classified as an illustration.

Illustrations are most likely to be included in non-fiction books or in children's books. With these two genres of writing, it is often useful to include illustrations as they can significantly enhance the appeal of a specific book to a reader.

Be sure to provide copies of the illustrations that you wish to include in your book to either the self-publishing company that is supporting the publication of your manuscript or to the printing house that will be printing copies of your book. It is important that this information is provided early on, so that the number of pages that your book will be can be determined, and that the print quality of your illustrations can also be assessed.

Finally, remember that as a self-publishing author it is your responsibility to get permission to include in your book any illustrations that aren't your own from the illustration'(s') owner. Be sure to have written confirmation of this permission, and to let the owner know how their illustration has been used within your book.

'As a self-publishing author it is your responsibility to get permission to include in your book any illustrations that aren't your own from the illustration'(s') owner.'

# Summing Up

- There are five key areas to consider when preparing your manuscript for publication. These areas are; obtaining feedback from individuals that you trust, copy editing your manuscript, proofreading your manuscript, typesetting your manuscript and managing book illustrations. Each of these areas can be approached methodically and external professionals should be used where possible to complete each of these key tasks.

- By spending time and energy at this preparatory stage, you should find that you save crucial time and money in the long run.

# Chapter Four

# That All-Important Book Cover

I think we've all heard the saying, 'don't judge a book by its cover'. Yet that is exactly what the majority of readers do. When we enter a bookstore or a library, unless we have entered the building in search of a specific book, the book we ultimately choose to read is likely to be one that was initially visually appealing. Therefore, as a self-publishing author, it is important that you spend some time creating a cover design for your book that will appeal to your identified audience.

## Why book covers are important

Book covers are important for a number of reasons. It is helpful to consider how a book cover can influence the sales figures for your books before settling on a final design.

- Often individuals will buy a book because they find the cover jacket eye-catching. If your book cover is plain, the likelihood is that a potential customer will quickly bypass your book in favour of another title which they believe looks like a better read.

- Clever or successful book covers engender a feeling of attachment with a reader. If a book cover reflects the spirit of the book itself, then the reader can become emotionally attached to the cover design.

- A book cover can influence how a reader 'reads' the text. The way that a character is drawn on the front cover of the book, for example, will force the reader to view this character in a certain way as they read through the story.

'It is important that you spend some time creating a cover design for your book that will appeal to your identified audience.'

- An attractive and intriguing book design will generally heighten the reader's sense of anticipation and excitement – they will feel that if the book cover is exciting then the text held on the pages of the book will be exciting too.

- Remember that whilst the imagery or visuals found on the front of a book jacket might be the first thing that catches the eye of a potential buyer, it is the blurb on the back of the book that introduces the story or contents to them that will ultimately influence their decision to (or to not) buy the book. It is therefore important that this is a well written and enticing section of text too.

## Choosing an image

Almost all book covers are made up of at least one image, and indeed many covers have a number of images that are placed on both the front and the back of the book jacket. Identifying the image or images that you want to use on your book cover is therefore a good place to start when designing your book jacket.

Any image used on your book cover should clearly and accurately express the primary message or theme of your book. It may be that your book is a romantic fiction piece; in which case you need an image that portrays the theme of this romance. Is the story one of forbidden love? Of unrequited love? Of a lost love? How can this specific form of romance be depicted through imagery on the book's cover? Remember that simple, direct images work best on a book jacket as they quickly create a focal point and can be easily interpreted.

It is also important to consider your targeted readership when choosing imagery for your book cover. Think about the age group, religion, ethics, and background of the individuals that are likely to read your book and ensure that your chosen imagery is sufficiently sensitive and respectful of their views. In addition, remember that your cover design should appropriately reflect the content of your book. Thus, if your book is a non-fiction, technical text, it would be best to steer away from comical designs or clip art style imagery as these do not reflect the professional and researched element of your book.

## Copyright rules and regulations

Under the Copyright, Designs and Patents Act 1988, all imagery including photography, drawings, diagrams, maps and logos, belong to the individual who first created the image in question. The image is therefore protected under copyright law, and no other person can lawfully copy the image or use the image themselves unless they have the permission of the image owner to do so.

Therefore, when choosing images to use on your book cover, be sure to only select images where the owner of the image has agreed that the image can be used by others, as part of a book production.

## Enticing readers

So, now you've considered the use of any imagery on your book cover, the next step is to consider the fuller design of the book cover itself. Below are some crucial steps to follow to help you do just that:

- Think about the key messages of the book. The book cover should reflect the key themes or key messages of the book. This might be achievable simply through the image that will appear on your front cover. However, often the font type you choose, your colour scheme and even the positioning of any imagery on the front and back covers of your book will also need to reflect your title's key theme. For example, if your book is a piece of romantic fiction, you'll be looking to use fresher colours and a rounder font type than you would choose for say a horror or science fiction novel.

'Balance is important.'

- Balance is important. Too many images can make a book cover look messy and uninviting. Similarly, the use of images that are too small or too infrequent can lead to too much empty space. When designing a book cover, your aim is to help your book stand out as much as possible, in a positive way. The individual elements of a book cover therefore need to work together to grab the attention of a potential reader, and convince them to study your book in greater detail. To achieve this, the elements of a book cover need to be arranged effectively – the final book cover should be pleasing and should promote easy eye flow.

- Font styles help the reader focus. Fancy font styles can make a book cover appear messy and can be off-putting to a potential reader. It is therefore important that you choose a font type that is clean and easy to read.

## The book blurb

Generally speaking, when it comes to book cover design, the focus is placed on the design of the front cover. However, most people spend more time reading and looking at the back cover of a book than they spend reviewing a book's front cover. Therefore, whilst the front of a book jacket must help to grab the attention of a potential reader, the information contained on the back of the book (aka the *book blurb*) will help the reader decide whether or not the book is worth a read.

'The colours you choose to use on your book cover depend on the emotions you intend to evoke in your readers.'

The information contained in a book blurb will vary from genre to genre, and different printers or self-publishing companies will have their own rules on how long a book blurb should be and what information it should contain. However, in general you will be looking to include the following pieces of information:

- An introduction to the main storyline and the lead character.

- Information on the author; for example, a picture of the author, a brief biography of the author's skill and writing experiences.

- One or two positive testimonials from previous readers.

## Choosing colours

The colours you choose to use on your book cover depend on the emotions you intend to evoke in your readers. In addition, certain colours suit certain title areas or book genres better. For example, lighter, pastel colours are quite calming and are therefore generally used on the book cover of self-help books or books that are specifically aimed at female readers.

The table opposite lists the colours that are best suited to particular book themes. Locate the theme that your book title fits into and then take a look at the colour pallet that best suits that theme. Does the image(s) you've chosen for your book work well with this colour scheme? Think about how you can use the listed colours to compliment the design of your book cover.

| Book theme | Suggested book cover colours |
|---|---|
| Antique | Brown, dark orange, mustard, tan, green, white, grey, silver |
| Classy | Black, gold, tan, purple, maroon, blue, mustard, orange, red |
| Comforting | Blue, white, orange, mustard, yellow, tan |
| Cool | Blue, purple, dark orange, yellow, silver |
| Corporate | Blue, grey, green, silver, black, purple, yellow, dark orange, white, grey, gold |
| Exciting | Green, red, orange, yellow, blue, purple, white |
| Feminine | Light yellow, green, lavender, light blue, purple, pink, white, plum, teal |
| Food | Green, brown, orange, purple, dark red, yellow, white, tan |
| Fresh | Light green, tan, yellow, orange, red, |
| Fun/Happy | Blue, yellow, dark pink, orange, red, turquoise, green, white |
| Healthy | Green, orange, purple, yellow, white |
| Masculine | Black, dark orange, blue, dark green, brown, tan, gold, red, grey |
| Modern | Blue, yellow, grey, purple, silver, green, orange, white, teal |
| Natural | Blue, brown, green, tan, yellow, mustard, tan |
| Rich | Black, maroon, grey, yellow, gold, green, sage, orange |
| Powerful | Black, orange, purple, red, yellow, blue, green, white, silver, grey |
| Warm/Hot | Dark green, red, orange, mustard, yellow |

Once you have identified which colours work best for your book type, you next need to choose the three or four colours from this list that you'd like to use on your book cover. Using any more than three or four colours on a book cover is likely to leave the cover looking busy and unprofessional. If you are using a coloured image on the book cover then aim to use just one or two colours throughout the rest of the cover, and choose colours that set off the image in a complementary way.

## Including quotations

You will often see quotations included on book covers. The quotations will be from previous readers of the book and they will be there to demonstrate why the book is worth a read. It is therefore useful to include quotations on your book cover, as they can convince potential readers that the book is definitely worth reading.

If possible, aim to include two or three short quotations on your book cover; one on the front of the book and one or two on the back of the book jacket.

Consider the following when seeking quotations to include on your book jacket:

'It is useful to include quotations on your book cover, as they can convince potential readers that the book is definitely worth reading.'

- You don't want your book jacket to appear too busy. Therefore quotations need to be as short and snappy as possible. Keep them to a sentence in length.

- Quotations should always be positive!

- Quotations need to be attributed to the individual who provided the feedback. The more renowned the individual providing the quotation, the better.

- Don't forget to seek written permission to print the quotation from the individual who provided the feedback to you.

## Completing the book design process

With images sourced, font types and colours determined, the book blurb written and feedback quotations identified, all that's left to do now is combine these elements to produce an enticing cover design! Easier said than done. Designing a book cover takes time as you work through a trial and error process. Your book cover needs to look great in a bookstore and also stand out as a tiny digital image on online bookseller websites. If you are working with a self-publishing company or a printing company that specialises in printing books, it is worthwhile seeking their input when finalising your cover design.

The book cover design process is outlined opposite in seven steps. Work through each step in sequence to help you settle on a book jacket design that works for you.

| Step 1 | Identify key themes | Identify what the key point of your book is. Also determine what attitude you want your front cover to express, i.e. professional or relaxed, and understand the desired audience for your book. |
|--------|--------------------|----------------------------------------------------------------------------------------------------------------------------------------------------------------------------------------------------|
| Step 2 | Complete your research | Take a look at other books that are of a similar genre to yours. Which covers do you like? Which don't you like? Why? |
| Step 3 | Collate ideas | Brainstorm your ideas for your book cover design. Write down anything and everything that comes into your head. |
| Step 4 | Prioritise your ideas | Which ideas from your brainstorm do you like best? How can you develop these further? |
| Step 5 | Draft your concept | Create mock-up book covers of your ideas. You can do this roughly yourself in Microsoft Word, or alternatively you can collaborate with a professional designer. |
| Step 6 | Test your favourites | Share your mock-up book covers with others. Test their reactions. Do they like the use of imagery? Is the text easy to read? Are the images strong enough? Does the colour scheme work? |
| Step 7 | Revise and refine | Revise your drafted jacket covers in light of the feedback received. |

# Summing Up

- The cover of a book is hugely important. It entices individuals to pick the book up and consider it as a potential read or purchase, it helps the reader visualise the theme, genre and content of the book, and it enables the reader to form an emotional attachment to the book itself. As a self-publishing author, it is therefore important that you spend time considering and planning the design of your book jacket.

- There are seven key steps to designing a book cover. The principle theme of the book should be first considered, and images that match that theme should be identified. Next, a colour scheme and font type that accentuate selected imagery should be determined. With this information to hand, ideas for a book cover can be brainstormed, prioritised and shortlisted. Mock-ups of each shortlisted book cover can then be created and tested on a selected audience to obtain feedback. Once this feedback has been received and appraised, a final book cover design can be created.

# Chapter Five

## Using a Self-Publishing Company

As identified in chapter 2 – The Different Routes to Self Publication, there are two principle ways to turn your manuscript into a purchasable book; through the use of a self-publishing company, or by independently managing the publication of your book yourself. Let's start by looking in detail at what you can expect if you decide to enlist the services of a self-publishing company to turn your manuscript into a complete book title.

'What can you expect from your self-publishing company?'

## What information will the self-publishing company need from me?

One you have identified the self-publishing company that you are going to work with, and have signed that all-important writer's contract (see chapter 2 – The Different Routes to Self Publication), the next thing you'll need to do is provide your chosen company with as much information as possible to enable them to create the perfect book for you.

The table overleaf outlines the type of information a self-publishing company will need from you, the author, to help them turn your manuscript into a published book. Use this information as a checklist, ensuring that you have all of these pieces of documentation or information compiled together and ready to send on to your chosen self-publishing company.

'Almost all books contain a "blurb" on their back cover which introduces the reader to the contents of the book.'

| Information Type | Description |
|---|---|
| Signed copy of the writer's contract | You will be issued with a standard contract by the self-publishing company (see chapter 2 – The Different Routes to Self Publication). Ensure that you sign and return this; having photocopied it first for your own records. |
| Full manuscript | It is very likely that the self-publishing company will have specific guidelines on how they need your manuscript to be provided to them. It will need to be available in an electronic format, normally typed into Microsoft Word. You should also receive instructions from the company on font type and size, line and paragraph spacing, and margin sizes. Be sure to format your manuscript to meet these instructions prior to sending the manuscript to them. |
| Author biography | An author biography can be used in many ways by your chosen self-publishing company. A small outline of your writing experiences to date, or of the experiences that qualify you to write on your chosen subject matter, will often be included on the back cover of your book. In addition, information about your local community, your social network, your qualifications and your experiences as a writer can be helpful when pulling together a marketing plan to publicise your printed book (see chapter 7 – Marketing Your Book). |
| Author photo | A photo of you, the author, may be requested by the self-publishing company for inclusion on the back cover of your book, or indeed to support your book's listing with distribution companies or to help with the initial marketing of your book. |
| Back cover book blurb | Almost all books contain a 'blurb' on their back cover which introduces the reader to the contents of the book (see chapter 4 – That All-Important Book Cover). This small section of text is usually between 200 and 300 words in length and will need to be prepared by you in advance of the book going to print. |

| Drafted ideas/ proofs for your book cover | A self-publishing company is likely to have an in-house design team that can create a book cover design for you. You may, however, want to present some draft ideas, images or style guidelines on how you'd like the jacket design of your book to appear. Provide images in a high resolution to ensure that the quality of the image is retained in the book cover design, and be as specific as possible on the shades of colours you'd like to see used. |
|---|---|
| Information to support the marketing of your book | It is unlikely that a self-publishing company will provide a book marketing service as a standard part of your contract with them; however many now offer marketing services to self-publishing authors, at an additional cost. If you do choose to purchase their marketing services then it is likely that you will need to provide the following information:<br><br>▪ Contact details for your local press.<br><br>▪ Details of any reading or writing groups in your local area.<br><br>▪ Details of any groups or societies that would take an interest in your book.<br><br>▪ Your availability for the completion of press interviews, book signings and book readings.<br><br>▪ A quotation from you on your experiences of writing and publishing the book in question. |

# What can I expect from my chosen self-publishing company?

Once you've provided your chosen self-publishing company with the information they need, you will be handing over responsibility for your book production to them. This is a big step for any author, as you will have dedicated months and sometimes even years of love, time and commitment to the completion of your manuscript, and now the future fate of that manuscript lies in someone else's hands.

By choosing a specific self-publishing company, by signing a contract with them and in many cases, by paying for their services, you should be able to expect to receive well-formatted, clearly printed books that reflect high-quality book production. These books should be available for distribution to booksellers and for direct purchase.

However, before your books are finally produced, you should receive ongoing communication from your chosen self-publishing company, updating you on how the production of your book is progressing. You should also receive proofs of your book for you to review in terms of text positioning, text accuracy and page formatting.

Listed below are a number of documents and communication topics that you should be able to expect from your chosen self-publishing company. If you are concerned that the company you've chosen to work with doesn't appear to be providing you with sufficient information or communication, be sure to raise this issue with them. And remember, you are not obliged to complete the final production of your book with them if you are unhappy with the initial provision of their services.

- Draft ideas of cover designs for your book, based on any specific images, illustrations or colours you may have previously provided.

- Revised versions of the drafted cover designs, following your feedback.

- Hard and electronic copies of your book proofs for you to check through. Proofs should reflect the proposed final formatting of your book so that you can check that you are happy with page layout.

- Revised versions of the book proofs, following your feedback or proofreading corrections. Revised book proofs should continue to be issued to you until you are happy with the quality and content of the proofs themselves.

- Copies of any marketing information regarding your book that will be circulated.

- Copies of the text used when listing your book with distributors or in the self-publishing company's own publication directory.

- Ongoing communication, on at least a fortnightly basis, outlining progress to date with your book production.

# Timescales and timelines

The amount of time it will take for a self-publishing company to turn your manuscript into a full and purchasable book will vary depending on the company used. It will also vary a little depending on the workload of your chosen self-publishing company – sometimes they will have a lot of books that require publication at the same time – other times they will be a little quieter.

On average, it takes six to eight weeks for a self-publishing company to turn your initial manuscript into a printed book. There is, however, a number of factors that can make this process a little more time-consuming. These factors include:

- The length of the manuscript.
- The level of internal imagery, diagrams or photography contained within the manuscript.
- How prescriptive the author is with regard to the design of the book cover.
- The number of changes made to the book proofs provided.
- The frequency of changes made to the book proofs provided.

## The self-publishing timeline

Overleaf is an indicative timeline which demonstrates the self-publishing process. The timescales provided for the completion of each step are based on the average amount of time it takes to create a self-published book, and so will vary for each author.

'On average, it takes six to eight weeks for a self-publishing company to turn your initial manuscript into a printed book.'

# Cost

It won't surprise you that the cost of self publishing your book varies considerably depending on (a) the type of book that you are looking to publish (hardback, paperback, etc.), (b) the self-publishing company you have chosen to use, (c) the amount of graphical input required to create the book, and (d) the length of the book. All of these factors have an impact on the cost of your

| | |
|---|---|
| Documentation required by self-publishing company (i.e. full manuscript and book blurb) provided by author | *1 week following contract agreement* |
| Page setting and manuscript formatting completed by self-publishing company | *3 weeks following contract agreement* |
| Proofs of manuscript sent to author for checking and proofreading. Draft book cover options created by self-publishing company | *4 weeks following contract agreement* |
| Manuscript proofs checked and proofread by author and returned to self-publishing company. Feedback on book cover options provided to self-publishing company | *3 weeks following contract agreement* |
| Manuscript proofs and book cover drafts revised in line with feedback and sent back to the author for approval | *5 weeks following contract agreement* |
| Author checks through revised documents and provides self-publishing company with approval | *6 weeks following contract agreement* |
| ISBN number allocated and author's copies of printed books provided. Marketing services (if agreed) commence | *7 weeks following contract agreement* |

book production. A hardback book, for example, will cost more to produce than a paperback book. In addition, the more pages a book has and the more complicated the imagery, the higher the production costs.

Some self-publishing companies still charge thousands of pounds to turn a manuscript into a published book. This usually represents an unnecessary expense and nowadays it is possible to use a self-publishing company to produce a book for a significantly lower cost. On average, the cost of self publishing a paperback novel with minimal imagery of less than 80,000 words is £600.

The website www.writersservices.com has a cost calculator for self-publishing authors to use. This can be very helpful when looking to estimate the average cost of self publishing your novel.

Using this calculator, we can see that the average design cost of a standard 250-page paperback is £375. Add to that the publication costs for a book of this type and length (£280) and the final average cost is £655. This cost could be reduced further if the design of the book cover was completed solely by the author.

As with all expenditures in life, it is useful to keep a safety net of funding when working out your self-publication budget. If possible, keep aside an additional 25% of the quoted publication cost to cover any unexpected extras that you might decide to take advantage of, such as the inclusion of preliminary pages, or additional graphics.

'As with all expenditures in life, it is useful to keep a safety net of funding when working out your self-publication budget.'

## Outcome – your final printed book

If you have been actively involved in the creation of your self-published book, the chances are that when the final version of the book is presented to you, you'll be happy with the outcome. Holding a copy of your very own book title in your hands for the first time is such a wonderful feeling – that sense of pride, success, achievement and anticipation all hit you at the same time.

Most self-publishing companies will provide you with a printed copy of your book for you to keep and cherish. This means that you will have an opportunity to review the final printed product before the book is made available to others for purchase.

## What to do if you are unhappy with the final product

If you are unhappy with the print or publication quality of your final book, then the best way to resolve this concern is to raise it verbally with the senior individual you have been liaising with at the self-publishing company.

Before speaking with them, be sure to have collated all of the information you need to support your complaint. You need to be able to provide evidence that your printed book does not reflect the product that you had been led to believe you would receive. Evidence in support of this would include:

- Sample copies of books that the company had previously printed that are similar to your book requirements and that demonstrate a higher quality of print.

- Drafts or proofs of your manuscript that the self-publishing company provided to you during the production stage, and that depict a higher standard of quality or accuracy than the final product.

- Any promotional information about the quality of books produced by the self-publishing company that was provided to you before or after you signed a contract with the company.

If your complaint cannot be resolved through a verbal discussion, put forward your case in a written formal complaint to the company, following their complaints process. By raising your concerns formally, the company is obliged to respond to you as proactively and efficiently as possible.

# Next steps

With your manuscript successfully turned into a book that can be sold, read and reviewed, your next step is to get it out there in the public domain for friends, family and your intended audience to purchase and read. A dedication to hard work and enthusiasm is a must as you embark on the promotional and marketing tasks that will help highlight your book as a 'must read' to local, national and international audiences.

# Summing Up

- If you choose to enlist the support of a self-publishing company to enable the production of your book, it is important that you provide them with the full manuscript, any ideas for a cover design and the text to be included on the back of the book jacket as quickly as possible. This will enable the company to provide you with the first set of book proofs in an efficient manner.

- A self-publishing company should work in an iterative way; providing you with copies of your book proofs to review before sending your book to print. Book production would normally take about 6 weeks, however be sure to finalise timescales and costs with a self-publishing company before signing a contract with them.

# Chapter Six
## Going It Alone

If you've decided against using a self-publishing company to support the creation of your self-published book, then you have the exciting task of managing the full publication process yourself. This might seem daunting initially, but organisation and a clear plan of action will enable you to create that perfect book, in a way that represents your enthusiasm and passion for writing and your dedication to your own written text.

When it comes to planning the publication process for your book, there are some crucial tasks that you need to consider. These include:

- Buying an ISBN number for your book.
- Sourcing a printing company to print the required copies of your book.
- Deciding on the quality of the final printed book copies.
- Arranging distribution methods for your book.
- Deciding how to stock, store and sell your book.

Let's look at each of these tasks in turn.

'Organisation and a clear plan of action will enable you to create that perfect book.'

## ISBN allocation

All books that are to be sold or stocked in bookstores or that are to be made available for sale through online shops should have an ISBN. The term 'ISBN' stands for International Standard Book Number. Since the beginning of 2007, ISBN numbers have contained 13 digits. Each independent book title is allocated its very own ISBN number which is unique to that specific book title, variation or edition. This therefore means that when a book title or edition needs to be located, it can be found via its ISBN.

It is therefore very important to you as a self publisher that you purchase an ISBN for your book title. If a bookstore or an individual wants to purchase a copy of your book, the best way for them to locate a copy and order it from either yourself or a distributor is to provide the ISBN that relates to your book title. Similarly, if a reader wants to locate your book in their local library for example, they will be able to do so by searching on the book's ISBN.

Furthermore, the ISBN of a book provides instant access to bibliographic databases, such as BookFind Online. These databases are organised by using the ISBNs of books as the key reference point. As these types of databases are used routinely by booksellers and libraries to provide information to customers on book recommendations or choices, they therefore act as a marketing tool and could help increase the number of book sales you achieve. The ISBN for your book therefore also acts as a promotional tool and can increase the readership of your title.

'The ISBN of a book provides instant access to bibliographic databases, such as BookFind Online.'

Self-publishing companies will often allocate an ISBN to a book title themselves. However, as an author choosing to self publish your book independently, this is a task that you must complete yourself.

## How do I obtain an ISBN for my book?

ISBNs can be ordered from the UK ISBN Agency, which is the national agency for the UK and Republic of Ireland. The UK ISBN Agency is run by Nielsen BookData UK.

The UK ISBN Agency sells ISBNs in batches. You can therefore choose to purchase a batch at a size that best meets your requirements. Most self-publishing authors would start by purchasing a small batch of ISBNs. Then, if they choose to write a significant number of new titles, a larger batch of numbers can be ordered.

Below is a list of ISBN batches and the costs relating to these batches. This information has been taken from the ISBN Agency's website (www.isbn. nielsenbook.co.uk) and these prices were correct at November 2011:

| Service | Description | Price |
|---|---|---|
| ISBN prefix for 10 numbers | Publisher registration, allocation of ISBN prefix plus a list of all 10 associated ISBNs. The list is issued by email or can be posted if required, at no extra fee. | £118.68 |
| ISBN prefix for 100 numbers | Publisher registration, allocation of ISBN prefix plus a list of all 100 associated ISBNs. The list is issued by email or if required, can be posted for an extra fee. | £222 |
| ISBN prefix for 1,000 numbers | Publisher registration, allocation of ISBN prefix plus a list of all 1,000 associated ISBNs. The list is issued by email or if required, can be posted for an extra fee. | £576.48 |
| Fast-track Processing | Processing time (from receipt of legible, fully and correctly completed application form with correct payment to issuing of ISBN prefix and numbers) is reduced from 10 working days to 3 working days. | £62.40 |
| Printing and posting of ISBN allocation | Additional fee payable for allocations of 100 or 1,000 ISBNs when issued by post. | £19.92 |

It is important to receive details of the ISBN that you are going to allocate to your book before the final book design is finalised with the printers, as you will need them to add these numbers, and the graphical representation of the ISBN (i.e. the barcode) to the back cover of your book.

To order a batch of ISBNs from the UK ISBN Agency, you simply need to complete an application form, which can be found online, and post, email or fax the application form and required payment information to Nielsen Books (details found on their website).

Your allocated ISBNs will then be provided to you by email or post. The standard turnaround time is 10 days, but as the table demonstrates, there is a fast-track 3-day option if required.

So, with the ISBN determined for your book, the next step is to identify a printing company who can turn your cover design and manuscript into a beautifully printed book.

## Sourcing a printer

There are thousands of printing companies across the UK and beyond who will be able to offer a service that enables them to print copies of your book for you. With so much choice, how do you know which printing company is the best one for you?

When it comes to self publishing, the best way to print your book is through a print on demand (POD) printing method. This means that books are printed as and when an order is placed for them. Printing in this way means that:

- Money isn't wasted. You don't need to spend money printing copious number of books that you can't then sell.

- Storage isn't an issue! As books are only printed to meet demand, you don't need to worry about where printed and unsold books need to be stored.

- You can still make a profit by printing in bulk. A print on demand solution means that if you know that there is a demand for a number of copies of your book (i.e. to sell at a planned launch party, etc.), then you can place a larger order with the printer and ultimately pay less per printed book than you would do if only one or two copies of the book were to be printed.

So, when narrowing down your search for a printer, start by looking for companies that can offer a strong POD package.

Next, think about the type of book that you have written. Is there anything special about this book that will impact on the way in which it is printed? Does it need a hard cover for example? If so, you'll probably find that a large number of potential printers are no longer viable as they cannot manage hardcopy books. Does your book contain a large amount of coloured print? Again, this may reduce your pool of printing companies or it may significantly increase the printing costs provided by some printers.

Having pulled together a list of printers that can offer a print on demand (POD) printing method and who can meet your specific book printing and formatting requirements, you now need to decide which of these shortlisted printing companies will work best for you and your book. Below are a series of points that you should consider when finally choosing a printing company for your book. Think through each of these points carefully – it may even be worth discussing these points with your shortlisted printers before you make your final decision.

- How much are the 'upfront costs' and what do these costs cover?

- How much will it cost for you to purchase copies of your own book (i.e. author copies)?

- Do they provide any input or requirements with regard to pricing the book to buyers?

- Can they provide examples of books that they have printed before in order to demonstrate print quality?

- How long does it take to print copies of the book once an order has been placed?

- Will they help you list your book with distributors such as Bertrams or with online sellers such as amazon.co.uk or play.com?

- Can they finalise or sharpen your drafted book cover to ensure maximum visual quality?

'Your chosen printing company should have lots of experience of working with self-publishing authors.'

## Paper, binding and finish

Your chosen printing company should have lots of experience of working with self-publishing authors. When it comes to deciding upon the paper, binding and finish of your book, their advice and guidance is invaluable. After all, this is their area of specialised knowledge!

## Paper

As stated in chapter 2 of this guide, the two principle print technologies used to produce books are digital and lithography. Normally, digital printing is more cost-effective if you are looking to produce between 300 and 500 copies of your book; for print runs larger than 500, lithography is often a more cost-effective approach. Lithography also tends to reproduce photos and other coloured images in finer detail; so if your book contains a lot of imagery then lithography might just be the best option for you. The best way to choose between the two print options is to ask a printer to produce a couple of pages of your book using the two different print technologies. Then decide from there.

Once you have decided which type of print technology you will use, the next step is to determine the quality and type of paper that each copy of your book will be printed on. Again, this is an area that your printing company will be able to assist with. The majority of paperbacks produced are printed on paper that is 80gsm (grams per square metre). You could however choose paper that is anything up to 170gsm. The higher the gsm of the paper, the thicker the pages, and thus the thicker the final copy of the book.

Different paper types may cost differing amounts, so keep your own budget in mind when determining the gsm of the paper you choose. After all, it is unlikely that a reader will be put off from ordering your book because they feel that the paper is too thin!

## Binding and finish

Book binding is an ancient skill and in many ways a form of art itself. Now that binding machines are available, binding a book together has become a relatively pain-free task. The most common forms of book binding are; saddle stitching, paperback binding and hardcover binding.

Saddle stitching is predominately used to bind leaflets and notepads, and so is only really suitable for small or thin books. Saddle stitched books are simply stapled twice or thrice in the centre.

Paperback binding is used for all paperback books. The spine of the book's pages is coated in glue twice before the spine is then placed into the book's constructed cover.

Hardback binding is used on chunkier books that have a solid, hardback book jacket. A similar process to paperback binding is followed, however an additional piece of fabric or card is glued or sewn onto the spine of the book's pages to provide additional strength.

If your book is to have a hardback book jacket then you will need to ensure that the printing company you've chosen uses a hardback binding method to ensure that the book has a professional finish and to ensure that the cover does not easily come apart from the rest of the book. If you have chosen to produce a paperback book, unless the book is very slim you will need to opt for a paperback binding option.

## Knowing how many to print

As discussed previously, the beauty of print on demand (POD) technology is that you only ever need to print as many books as you know you will sell.

For books that are purchased directly from a bookseller or supplier, this process is easy. A book order comes in to the printer, following the request of a customer. The printer prints and binds the books ordered and distributes to the customer.

However, it may be that you are holding a book launch, series of book readings or you may want to provide copies of your book as presents to friends and family. In these instances, you can request that the printing company prints a greater number of books for you.

Be careful not to print too many books for occasions such as these. It is best to estimate the number of copies you think you'll need for the events that you know you have scheduled; don't be tempted to waste money by ordering more copies than needed with the hope that you'll sell all copies eventually. Instead, approximate how many individuals will attend the events that you have planned. Then order one and a half or two times this number. By acting this way you should have just the right number of book copies to sell at your promotional events.

'The beauty of print on demand (POD) technology is that you only ever need to print as many books as you know you will sell.'

# Distribution

When you purchase your ISBNs from Nielson, they will automatically add your book title to their distribution database. This means that if a bookstore uses Nielson as the company that provides them with all of their book stock, they will easily be able to order copies of your book. By approaching Gardners and Bertrams, other large distribution companies, you can also have your book title added to their distribution collection (see Chapter Ten: Help List). Similarly, amazon.co.uk will allow you to list your book with them; enabling readers to purchase your book online.

You can of course also sell copies of your book yourself; either at book fairs, at promotional events that you have organised to market your book, or even online, through your own website. The possibilities are endless.

## Stocking your books in local bookstores

'It is often best to approach a bookshop manager or owner in person.'

Owners of independent bookstores are often more than happy to support local authors by stocking copies of their publications. Similarly, local Waterstones' branches often agree to purchase copies of books that have been written by local authors.

Having your book on display in bookshops can make a big difference to your book sales. Whilst almost all bookstores have the ability to order a copy of your book into store for any customer who requests a specific book title, those readers who are not aware of your book will need to see a copy of your book in a bookstore before they can purchase and read the book. Convincing bookshop owners or managers to stock a number of copies of your book is therefore a very worthwhile exercise!

It is often best to approach a bookshop manager or owner in person; choose a day where the shop is generally quite quiet and take a copy of your book and a portfolio of any promotional material that you may have about the book with you. Introduce yourself to the bookstore manager or owner and explain that you are a local author, and that you would like a moment of their time to speak to them about your latest publication. On the whole, you should find that most of your local independent bookshops will be more than willing to stock several copies of your book.

Once a bookstore has agreed to stock copies of your book, you will need to agree with them the best way for them to obtain these copies. It is likely to be more cost-effective for you if they choose to purchase the books from you direct. However, they may prefer to order copies of the books through Nielsen, Gardners or Bertrams. If this is the case, be sure to provide them with the book's ISBN so that they can easily place an order.

## Storing your books

If you choose to have a large quantity of books printed for your own distribution purposes; i.e. to give to friends and family, to sell to local bookshops, to sell at book fairs, or to sell at book launches or readings, then you will need to think about where and how to store copies of your book.

There are two main options; store them in your own home or the home of a very helpful friend/family member, or pay for some form of storage space.

Storing books in your own home is often the best solution when you have less than 100 copies of the book to store. It means that you don't have to incur any storage costs, copies of your book are easily accessible and 100 books, when they are well stacked or boxed, shouldn't take up too much space. However, if you have more than 100 books to store, it might be worthwhile seeking out a specific storage unit for your books. Companies such as the Big Yellow Self Storage (www.bigyellow.co.uk) can provide storage units in all shapes and sizes, all around the country. Alternatively, speak to your printing company and see if they can help. Often printing houses will offer a storage solution to self-publishing authors, which means that once copies of your book have been printed, they can be stored with the printers, on site. If your printing company is local, this could well be the perfect solution to your storage conundrum!

# Summing Up

Managing the publication and printing of your own book is a wonderful achievement, and one that doesn't have to be stressful. By following an organised plan, you can quickly and efficiently turn your manuscript into a purchasable book. Remember to:

- Purchase an ISBN.

- Look to work with a POD printer.

- Source a printer who can meet the individual specifications of your book.

- Decide upon a paper type that is cost-effective and attractive.

- Use the easiest and most reliable binding method for your book.

- Add your book to distribution companies' records.

# Chapter Seven
# Marketing Your Book

## What is marketing?

There are lots of different definitions of 'marketing' out there. Different individuals and different companies define the term 'marketing' in a range of ways. Some of the best definitions of marketing include;

'Marketing is the social process by which individuals and groups obtain what they need and want through creating and exchanging products and value with each other' – *Kotler*

'Marketing is the management process that identifies, anticipates and satisfies customer requirements profitably.' – *CIM*

'The right product, in the right place, at the right time, at the right price.' – *Adcock*

'Marketing is essentially about marshalling the resources of an organization so that they meet the changing needs of the customer on whom the organisation depends.' – *Palmer*

All of these definitions have three key points in common.

- They all recognise that there needs to be a product or service that is being marketed.

- They all recognise that the product or service needs to appeal to the needs or desires of others (aka, the customer).

- They all recognise that 'marketing' is the means through which you bring the service or product to the customer in a way that meets their identified needs or desires.

'The right product, in the right place, at the right time, at the right price.'

Adcock

# Why is marketing important to self publishers?

As a self publisher, or an author who has published their own book, the next step of your journey is to make book sales – to get your book out there in the world and encourage others to read it and buy it. Even if the motivating factors sitting behind the creation of your self-published masterpiece were not financially driven, almost all authors want to have their work read by someone at some point. And so this is where marketing comes in. To introduce people to your book, to encourage them to spend time reading your book and to ultimately sell your book, you need to get your published writing out there in the public domain. It needs to be visual and accessible to your chosen audience. You therefore need to market your book at individuals who are likely to need to read your book, or have a desire to read your book. We'll call this group of people your 'targeted audience'.

Your targeted audience will be made up of a range of individuals who have a particular interest in the genre of book that you have written, or in the subject matter about which you have written. Let's look at an example to illustrate this.

Say you have written a non-fiction book on World War II. Who would be your targeted audience?

- Friends and family, people who you know personally and who want your book to do well.
- Your local community who like to read books written by others who live nearby.
- World War II veterans.
- Families of World War II veterans.
- Historians.
- History teachers.
- Literary students who are focusing on texts compiled during or about this period.
- History or humanity students.
- Others with a general interest in history.
- Members of history or World War II related societies or groups.
- The local press.

And no doubt there are many more.

These are the groups of people that you want to market your book at, as they are more likely to go on and read or purchase your book than, say, someone who has a real, keen interest in gardening, but who isn't particularly interested in historical events. In the next few sections of this chapter we'll look at ways in which you can market your book to your targeted audience.

Marketing is an important role that all writers have to undertake when it comes to promoting a book. For authors who have secured a traditional publishing deal, there may be some support in completing marketing exercises from an in-house marketing team, but for the valiant self publisher, this is often a task that has to be completed single-handedly. It is also traditionally harder for a self-published book to get exposure in magazines, newspapers and literary publications through book reviews or adverts, and so the role of marketing in promoting a self-published book becomes even more important. Marketing your book can, however, be the most exciting part of your publication journey! It involves talking about your book, celebrating its arrival into the literary world, and sharing it with others – all of which are enlightening and fulfilling activities (even if they seem somewhat daunting at times).

## How to market your book

There are so many ways to market a book, particularly when it comes to marketing your book to smaller or local audiences.

Your first considerations need to be time and resource availability. Promoting your book is going to involve a reasonable amount of time commitment on your part, and almost all of the activities will involve some financial investment and/or resource investment from others around you. The beauty of book promotion however, is that because there are so many different ways to market your book, you can always find a way that best suits you.

The grid overleaf contains a number of different promotional ideas that you can adopt to market your book. The ideas are pooled into 4 groups; low time commitment and low cost, low time commitment and high cost, high time commitment and low cost, and high time commitment and high cost. Use the grid to identify marketing ideas that would suit your time and resource availability.

'Marketing your book can be the most exciting part of your publication journey!'

| Low time commitment and low cost | Placing an advert in a local publication |
|---|---|
| | Completing an interview about your book |
| | Word of mouth |
| | Advertising your book on social networking sites |
| | Emailing a bulletin to let people know that your book is available for purchase |
| Low time commitment and high cost | Advertising your book in national publications |
| High time commitment and low cost | Book signings |
| | Book talks |
| | Completing articles on your book writing experience |
| | Speaking to local bookstores and libraries to ask them to stock your book |
| | Writing and circulating a press release |
| | Circulating review copies of your book |
| High time commitment and high cost | Hosting a launch party |
| | TV advertising |
| | Radio advertising |
| | Creating and distributing leaflets |

As an author marketing your book, you have the freedom and flexibility to choose which marketing ideas you want to implement and which just aren't right for you. That's the beauty of self publishing! From the grid above, and from your own additional thoughts and ideas, you can choose to undertake as many or as little marketing activities that suit your lifestyle and your book promotion ambitions.

A lot of authors choose to incorporate the writing and circulation of press releases, the distribution of review copies, the undertaking of book signings and the completion of book readings into their marketing plans. The rest of this chapter therefore explores these activities in greater detail, supporting you to include them into your own book marketing plans as required. Chapter 8 then goes on to looking at one of the bigger marketing events many self-publishing authors embark upon – throwing that all-important launch party!

## Press releases

Press releases are written to announce a new service or product. As their name suggests, they are traditionally sent to members of the press who would then decide if the announcement is sufficiently 'newsworthy' for them to publish in their individual publications.

Press releases are a great way to let the local press know that you have written a book, let them know what the book is about and give them an opportunity to alert their readers or listeners to the release of the book. As local radio stations, newsletters and newspapers tend to support their local community, you should find that they will read your press release with interest and will publicise the information as proactively as possible.

Press releases can also be distributed online. There are a number of press release distribution sites (see the help list) that will allow you to upload your press release to the website, and they will then send it out to hundreds of online publications. This enables you to reach a much greater global audience, signposting potentially thousands of individuals to your book.

So, what should go into a press release?

- It needs a snappy, catchy title to ensure that it grabs the attention of the reader.
- A press release should be no more than one page in length.
- The opening two paragraphs should detail the genre of the book, the main plot line, and include details of who you think will buy the book.
- A mini author's biography should be included.
- If possible, include a picture of your book within the press release to demonstrate how enticing the cover is and to add some colour.
- Your press release should have the ISBN number of the book on it, and details of how purchasers can buy the book.

'Press releases are a great way to let the local press know that you have written a book.'

## Distributing review copies of your book

Distributing review copies of your book involves identifying publications that will complete a book review for you, and who will subsequently publish their review. Book reviews are a handy marketing activity as they are predominately low cost and involve little time commitment. It is also found that individuals are more likely to buy a book if they read a good review about it, or if it is recommended to them.

If you are considering sending out review copies of your book to publications, it is important to remember the following:

'Book reviews are a handy marketing activity as they are predominately low cost and involve little time commitment.'

■ Only send review copies to publications that you know are likely to review your book. A lot of books have been wasted in the past by authors targeting the wrong type of publication. National magazines and national newspapers are extremely unlikely to review a self-published book. Very sad, but currently very true. Local magazines, newsletters and papers, however, are much more likely to undertake a review of a book that is sent to them by a local resident, so target magazines and newspapers from your local community first.

■ *The Self Publishing Magazine* (see the help list) reviews a wide range of books each quarter, and they have a pool of independent reviewers to complete the book reviews for them. Approach them and see if they will accept a copy of your book for review.

■ There are a number of printed and online publications for specific subject matters, such as gardening, bird watching, cars, cooking and baking. Think about how your book might appeal to a specific interest group and do some investigating to see if there are any publications aimed at these interest groups. Approaching these publications may lead to a printed positive review of your book!

■ It is important to send a cover letter with each review book you send out, explaining what the book is all about, why you think it would be of interest to that particular publication, and what you would like the recipient to do with the book (i.e. read and review it!).

## Book signings and readings

Book signings or book readings are a great way to get yourself and your book known to your targeted audience. However the prospect of actually completing a book signing, or even worse, reading out an extract of your book and talking to strangers about it can feel incredibly scary.

If you have decided that you want to include book signings and book readings into your marketing plan then ask yourself how much time you are willing to commit to these activities. If your time is limited, perhaps decide to first only complete a couple of signings and readings within your local community. If you have a greater amount of time available to you for book signings and readings, then find a map and start to identify locations where you can deliver your signings or readings. You could focus on towns within your county . . . or you could plan an entire road trip of the country! The choice is yours.

Regardless of how many signings or readings you plan to deliver, the planning process is the same. The checklist overleaf should help you work through each planning stage in a logical and successful way:

# Checklist for planning a book reading or signing

1.  Identify a location for your book signing or book reading event. Book signings are usually most successful when they are carried out in busy shopping or socialising areas such as a bookstore, a shopping mall, a supermarket, a café or a bar. Book readings, however, need a quieter space with an indentified audience such as a library, a book group, a society group (such as the W.I.) or a school assembly.

2.  Approach the manager of your chosen location. Try a courtesy call first and then arrange a time and date that would be convenient for you to meet and discuss your reading or signing plans.

3.  Draw up a list of the questions you have before your meeting. These questions might include,

    ▪ What promotional material can I bring on the day (posters, etc.)?

    ▪ Will there be a desk, chair and pens provided for me?

    ▪ Will there be any promotional material displayed or circulated prior to my signing/reading?

    ▪ How will I be able to sell my books?

    ▪ What time should I arrive?

    ▪ How long am I likely to be signing or reading for?

    ▪ How many people are likely to attend?

    Take a copy of your book and any promotional material you hope to display with you to the meeting with the location manager.

4.  Agree the details of the signing/reading, working through the list of questions you have. Make sure you leave the meeting knowing when and where you need to arrive on the agreed day of the signing/reading.

5.  Preparation is key! A few days prior to the reading or signing, ensure that you have everything you need for the day organised and packed up and ready to go! This may include; receipts to issue when selling your books, petty cash so that you can give customers any required change, promotional material, Blue-tack or pins for hanging posters, pens for signing books, your written and rehearsed reading, the books themselves!

6.  Work through all the practical arrangements for the day. How long will it take you to get to the desired location? Do you know the route? Where can you park your car?

7.  Make sure you have eaten something on the morning of the signing or reading, as this will give you energy and will help to calm any anxious tummy butterflies.

8.  Take a deep breath and smile as you enter the location. Remember, these people are here to see and listen to you!

# Summing Up

Marketing is an extremely important part of the publication process for self publishers, as it is the only real way of letting readers know that your newly created book is out there in the world, available for them to read and buy. Without the backing of an in-house marketing team that larger traditional publishing houses often have, it is up to you as the self publisher to organise marketing activities to promote your book. As you embark on this process, remember the following:

- Identify your target audience, so that you know who you should be aiming your marketing activities at.

- Review your time and resource availability before planning any marketing event, so that you can be sure that the marketing activities you've chosen to pursue fit with your lifestyle.

- It is easier to market your book through the use of local amenities such as radio stations, magazines, newsletters and newspapers than it is to try and tackle national publications.

- Interest groups may have subject-based magazines or newsletters that they read. Do a bit of research to see if you can find specialist publications that are relevant to your book. You can then promote your book to these publications via a press release or by sending them a review copy of your book.

- Book signings or readings are a great way to interact with your target audience.

- Decide how much time you have available to dedicate to a book signing or reading schedule. Then decide how many signings/readings you want to complete.

- Use the checklist provided in this chapter to ensure that each book signing or reading goes as smoothly and as positively as possible.

OK, now let's take a look at throwing your own book launch!

'Marketing is an extremely important part of the publication process for self publishers.'

# Chapter Eight
# Throwing Your Own Launch Party

As we saw in the last chapter, holding a launch party for your book is a great marketing tool that can be used to publicise your work and encourage more people to purchase and read your book. Holding a launch party is generally one of the more expensive and time-consuming marketing tools that can be used by authors to highlight their work. However, it is also a hugely rewarding and often very successful way to get your book out there in the public domain.

In this chapter, we'll look at the key stages involved in creating a successful launch party. By breaking down the party planning and hosting requirements into manageable tasks, you'll find that you can become a winning host or hostess, and that you'll enjoy fulfilling the role at the same time.

'Holding a launch party for your book is a great marketing tool.'

## Creating a plan

Organisation is the often deemed the 'key' to success and this has never been more true than when it comes to events management. So before you even think about calling the caterers in and locating that all-important book signing pen, you must spend some time with a blank sheet of paper and a pencil in order to create a party planner's 'plan of action'.

There are lots of different things you need to consider when it comes to throwing a launch party. In order to complete your plan of action, you'll need to work through each of the key tasks that need to be undertaken to enable the successful delivery of your launch party.

The checklist below identifies a range of tasks that need to be considered by any party planner. When it comes to organising your own launch party, use the list below to determine exactly which tasks you will need to undertake, and then determine the order in which these tasks need to be completed.

| Checklist for planning a launch party: Key tasks | |
|---|---|
| Agree a budget | Ensure copies of books are available |
| Locate a venue | Arrange transport for the event |
| Decide on the style of the party | Set up cash box for book purchases |
| Determine date and time of party | Purchase receipt book |
| Draw up a guest list | Arrange to arrive at venue early on day |
| Send out invitations | Purchase book signing pens |
| Locate food/drink provider | Identify outfit for the night |
| Determine menu | Purchase any extra marketing materials |

Once you have identified which of the key tasks need to be completed in order to plan your party, and you've decided in what order you need to complete each task, your next job is to identify who needs to complete each task, and by when. It may be that you are single-handedly taking on the role of party planner, or it may be that you have a few willing volunteers that you can rope in to support the planning process. Either way, by setting strict deadlines for the completion of each task you'll be able to guarantee that you're well organised on the day of the launch, which in turn will reduce your stress levels significantly and will help you enjoy the event itself.

# Finding a venue

One of the key tasks that is sitting on your action plan will be the need to determine a budget for the party. Setting a budget will help you narrow down all of the other choices you will need to make in terms of venue, catering and guest numbers. It is therefore important that you have determined a realistic budget for the party before you start looking at party venues, otherwise you could find yourself committing more money than desired to extravagant venue locations, as it is easy to get carried away when viewing different vicinities.

Having set a budget you should then think about the style of your party. Do you want the party to reflect the theme of your book for example, or would you like the venue to mirror the setting of your story? Are you looking for an elegant evening cocktail reception or would you prefer a daytime event with coffee and cake? All of these questions need to be asked and answered early on in the planning stage of your party, before the launch party venue is identified.

Once these important decisions about budget and style have been made, the next stage of your action plan is to choose a venue. You will be looking to choose a venue that is, importantly, within budget, that is appropriate for the style of your event and that is centrally located for the guests that you are planning to invite. The Internet is a very useful place to start your initial research as there are a number of websites that offer a free search facility for venues in the UK and internationally (see the help list). Don't limit yourself purely to places that advertise that they have function rooms or that can cater for private parties; if there is a particular venue that you are interested in but you're not quite sure if they'd be able to accommodate you, give them a call. You won't know unless you ask. Select a shortlist of five venues and, most importantly, visit each of them before you settle upon a final party location. The venue that you finally choose should compliment your book and your ideas for your party. It is important to note here that you do not always have to arrange a formal visit to a venue. If, for example, you are considering a bar or café as your launch party setting, why not pay them an unannounced visit during a busy period so that you can see first hand how they cope with large numbers, what their standard of customer service is like, and how strong the quality of their food and drink appears to be.

When visiting venues, either announced or unannounced, it is a good idea to run through a number of questions with the venue manager. These questions will help with the completion of the next stages of your action plan and will also help you rule in or rule out each venue that you view.

Good questions to pose when looking at venues include:

- Will you have exclusive use of the venue?
- Is the venue easily accessible for your guests?

'If there is a particular venue that you are interested in but you're not quite sure if they'd be able to accommodate you, give them a call.'

- Is the venue available for the time and date you have chosen?

- Can they provide catering in-house?

- Will you be allowed to bring in external caterers?

- Are the toilet facilities adequate?

- Will there be space to display your book?

- Will there be enough staff to cater for the number of intended guests?

Once you have weighed up the pros and cons of each of your shortlisted venues you should then be able to make your final decision. Remember that this is *your* event and the venue, style and theme should reflect you, your style and your book. It is important that you feel happy and at ease in the surroundings you have chosen.

## Compiling a guest list

Compiling a guest list is one of the most difficult stages of the planning process. You will no doubt want to ensure that your family and friends are invited to the party to celebrate the completion of your book with you. However, you will also want to invite a wider range of writers, readers and members of the local press to ensure that your book is given maximum exposure within the literary world.

It can be a good idea to split your guest list into 5 different categories; family, friends, writers, readers and press. The first two lists will be the easier to compile, but try and hold back with the numbers in these groups to ensure that you have an appropriate proportion of guests from the other groups. Fellow writers may be members of your own writing group but don't be afraid to contact other local writing groups, particularly if they have similar writing interests as your soon-to-be published book. A directory of writing groups in your area can be found on the Internet (see the help list), or you can visit your local library to obtain similar information. Always make telephone contact first to establish an appropriate named person to invite, to ensure that they would actually be interested and available to attend. Readers can be found via book clubs, which again are often associated with libraries. Be selective about the book groups that you approach as you are more likely to get a positive response to a book launch if it is the type of book that these groups are interested in reading.

Contacting the press may seem like a daunting experience but local newspapers are always keen to write about the success of a member of their local community so it is definitely worth giving their news desk a call and identifying a relevant reporter to invite to the launch. Similarly, try contacting your local radio show, or perhaps the editor of your local news bulletin and invite them along to the party – you'll find that this one event could well lead to you appearing on the local radio show as a guest interviewee or could provide content for a journalistic piece on your book appearing in a local publication.

Another venue to explore is organisations that may be interested in stocking your book, for example local independent bookstores, or schools and libraries. If your book belongs to the non-fiction genre, why not invite industry-specific representatives to attend your launch party?

To get an idea of the ratio that each of these groups of guests should contribute to your party; a suggested combination for a party of 50 guests should include, 16 family members, 16 friends, 8 writers, 8 readers and 2 press. A top tip when compiling your guest list is to create two lists, where one acts as a reserve. Therefore when you inevitably get some responses to your invitations that state that certain individuals are unable to attend, you'll have a backup to fill their place. Establishing this reserve list right at the start will avoid any panic during the later planning stages, when you should be enjoying accessorising your event.

Send your invitations out in plenty of time to give your guests adequate notice. Your invitations should reflect the style of your party and provide details of all of the arrangements for the event, including venue name and address, date, time, dress code and most importantly the purpose of the party: the launch of your new book! A good tip is to provide reply slips to take the hassle out of replying. This will ensure that you know definite guest numbers early on, and you won't then have to start calling and chasing people for their responses.

# Organising the catering

Now that the guests have been invited to your launch, and the party venue has been booked, it is time to start enjoying the designing, staging and finalising of the finer details of your event. One of these first areas of consideration is the catering requirements – exactly what food and drink provisions do you need to make?

'Contacting the press may seem like a daunting experience but local newspapers are always keen to write about the success of a member of their local community.'

There are a number of questions that you can ask yourself when considering your catering requirements which, once answered, will help you decide upon the food and drink provision required for the evening. Use the list of questions below to help you determine the catering arrangements for your launch party:

- What time is the event? Will guests be arriving straight from work and thus expect a large quantity of food? Would a finger buffet suffice? Or perhaps the event is to be held in the morning or afternoon, in which case a few nibbles and coffee would work perfectly.

- What is your budget for food and drink?

- Do you want to provide drinks to guests free of charge, or would you prefer for them to purchase their own beverages from a bar within the venue?

- Is catering provided by your chosen venue or will you need to source external caterers?

- Do you have any specific ideas about tying the food and/or drink provision in with the theme of the book? You could name a cocktail after one of the book characters for example, or have a motif from the book visualised through a food item.

Through answering the questions above you'll be able to determine the type of food and drink selection your party will provide. Your next step is to turn these decisions into a reality. The checklist of actions opposite will help you do this in an efficient and stress-free manner!

## The finer details

It is at the 'finer details' stage that most authors and party organisers get a little carried away and when firmly agreed budgets get blown!

There is always the pull to ensure that your launch party is unique in some way. It might be that you want to splash out and dress your venue slightly differently than it would normally appear, perhaps with some dramatic drapes or with some seating that helps to enhance your theme and desired style. Alternatively, you may want to have a number of promotional items available for guests to take away with them; perhaps something simple such as a pen with the title of your book written across it, or something a little more complex such as a personalised USB key. Some authors even choose to have goodie bags containing an array of items that are handed to guests at the end of the event.

There are lots of positive reasons for enhancing your launch party in order to make it as memorable as possible. However, it is important to remember that the party will be an awful lot less enjoyable for you if the final cost of the event is over budget. So, as you work through the finer details of your party organisation, be sure to keep a firm record of your expenses and frequently compare it to your budget. If you find yourself going over budget then be firm with yourself and make some cutbacks. It may even help to enlist the support of a friend or family member who you can trust to manage the budget for you.

---

### Checklist for organising launch party catering: Key tasks

- Ensure your food and drink budget is engraved in your mind!

- If catering isn't provided by the venue, draw up a shortlist of potential external caterers and speak to each company about your requirements before final selection.

- Collect sample menus from caterers, and ensure all sample menus provided are within your budget.

- Arrange a tasting session for the food and drink options proposed. Following this, finalise the menu.

- Ensure all practical issues have been clarified with the caterers; what time they will arrive on the night with the food, when the food and drinks will be provided to the guests, how the food and drink will be provided to the guests, when and how they will be paid, etc.

- Ensure you have a number of contact details for the caterers for the day of the event, in case you need urgent liaison with them.

---

'The party will be an awful lot less enjoyable for you if the final cost of the event is over budget.'

# The final 48 hours

As the date of your party draws near, keep in regular contact with your venue and a named person there who is involved with your party organisation. Organise a quick catch-up with your venue in the 48 hours before the event is scheduled to take place to review the 'on the day' arrangements once more and to finalise any last minute preparatory plans. Now is a good opportunity to establish an exact time that you can enter your venue and start to set up.

Use the last 48 hours before the party to confirm transport arrangements for the launch, to ensure that you are happy with catering timings, and to check your book stock. Ensure that you have all of the items that you'll be taking with you to the launch collected together. This might include business cards to hand out as part of your personal advertising, notepaper to allow you to collate the details of any connections, as well as pens for book signing, loose change and your receipt book. Finally, try on your launch party outfit one last time to ensure that you are happy and comfortable with your personal presentation.

# On the day!

The time to celebrate that your book has arrived! As guests arrive, take time to acknowledge and speak to everyone that has made the effort to attend. Remember that some of your guests may not know many other attendees, particularly representatives of any local reading or writing groups, so they may need extra attention to help them relax into the event. When speaking with the press let them know of your connections with the area and speak about your book, without giving the 'hard sell'. They are likely to ask you specific questions about your book and your inspiration behind its creation, so be prepared with some well thought out answers.

Possible questions you should prepare for include:

- Why did you decide to write this book?

- What was your inspiration for this book?

- Where can your book be purchased?

- Will there be any future marketing activities?

- What's next for you and your writing?

Once your launch is over, it is important that you keep the enthusiasm and momentum going. Follow up with your guests to thank them for coming, to confirm new contacts and to develop your writing network. Look at your launch party as the beginning of a successful journey for your book's position within the literary world.

## Summing Up

Hosting a book launch is a great way to market your book to the local community and to celebrate its completion and successful publication. However it takes strong organisational skills to deliver a triumphant launch party. Ensure you've pulled together a robust launch party 'action plan' in advance of the event which includes the following:

- Setting a realistic budget.
- Choosing a venue that works for you.
- Creating a guest list that includes friends, family, press contacts and representatives from local book and writing groups.
- Deciding upon food and drink provisions that meet the needs of the launch.
- Organising transport to and from the venue for you . . . and your books!
- Following up enthusiastically on all contacts after the launch to further increase the visibility of your book within the local area.

'Ensure you've pulled together a robust launch party 'action plan' in advance of the event.'

# Chapter Nine

## Royalties

Receiving financial recognition for your writing may not be the principle driving force behind your desire to self publish your manuscript. However, the majority of self-publishing authors welcome payment following the sale of their books. Whether your aim is to recoup the money you've spent on producing your book or indeed, to generate a profit through book sales, you'll need to understand how you receive payment for the books that you sell, and how these payments need to be recorded.

## What are royalties?

The term 'royalties' refers to the payments authors receive following the sale of one or more copies of their book. Royalty payments are usually calculated as a percentage of the book's selling price and, if someone else is managing the sale of your book, are paid in arrears.

### How do you receive royalties as a self-publishing author?

How you receive royalties from your books will differ depending on how you have chosen to print and sell your books. As we've discussed throughout this guide, there are two principle ways of approaching self publishing; using a self-publishing company or going it alone! Each approach in turn has a different way of providing royalty payments to self-publishing authors.

'You'll need to understand how you receive payment for the books that you sell, and how these payments need to be recorded.'

## Royalty payments – using a self-publishing company

If you've enlisted the support of a self-publishing company to produce your book, you'll no doubt have found that this company will also take on responsibility for printing and distributing your book to commissioning booksellers. This means that they will provide copies of your book to a bookstore that agrees to stock your title, and will manage any costs associated with this. They will then provide you with a royalty payment for any books sold during a set period, say every quarter. Your royalty payments may be provided to you via cheque, or by a payment made directly into your bank account by the self-publishing company. Either way, you should receive a statement at the same time that outlines how many copies of your book have been sold, who they have been sold to, and how the sum of your royalty payment has been derived.

## Royalty payments – going it alone

If you've decided against using a self-publishing company to support the production of your book, you'll need to take on responsibility for organising the printing, distribution and sales of your title. This therefore means that you'll have to agree a price at which copies of your book will be printed, you'll need to pay any distribution company that handles your book, and you'll need to negotiate the amount of money a bookseller will keep from the cover price of your book. Your royalty payment will then be the total of any sum of money left over from the sale of your books, once printers, distributors and sellers have been paid. This may seem a hugely daunting and complicated process, but, in reality, it is a case of remembering who needs to pay who . . . and when! The flow chart opposite demonstrates this payment cycle in a step-by-step manner:

84

Seller (i.e. book store) agrees a percentage cut off of the book price with the author.

Seller places order; either through distributor (i.e. Gardners) or direct with printers.

Printer prints books to fulfil order placed. Printer then invoices the author for the cost of printing the books.

Distributor passes books to seller. Distributor then invoices the author for the cost of distributing the books.

Author invoices seller for book provision at the agreed rate per book ordered.

Book is sold to the customer, who pays the seller.

'Each person involved in this process will want payment for the part that they play in ensuring the successful sale of your book.'

## What proportion of royalties do self-publishing authors receive?

There are a number of different people involved in the book production and transportation process; i.e. the process that moves your book from being a finalised, electronic manuscript to a printed book that is purchased by a reader. Each person involved in this process will want payment for the part that they play in ensuring the successful sale of your book. Only once these individuals have been paid will you be able to receive any royalty payment from the book sale.

The diagram below illustrates who might need to be paid from the money received through the sale of your book.

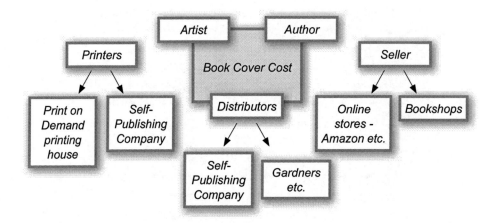

Depending on the publication approach you've taken, you'll either have enlisted the help of an independent printer to print each copy of your book that's purchased for you, or you'll have chosen a self-publishing company that will print a copy of your book for each order placed. Either way, it is likely that the printing element of the book production process will require circa 20% of the book cover price as payment.

Once printed, your book needs to make its way to the shop or store that is going to sell it. This process is known as distribution. If your book is being sold in a large bookstore such as WHSmith for example, it is likely that a company such as Gardners or Bertrams will be responsible for the distribution of your book to each of these stores.

The store that is selling the book for you will need to take a percentage of the book cover price as payment. Generally speaking, the distribution costs and the seller costs of a self-published book total 60%.

Finally, if you have used an artist to create the book cover or to produce imagery for the inside of the book, you may have agreed to pay them on a payment-per-book-sold principle as opposed to paying them fully upfront for the production of the artwork. If this is the case then you will need to factor in the artist's payment too. Given the costs outlined above that are payable to the printers, distributors and sellers, in order to achieve any royalty payment at all from the sale of each of your books, you would need to keep any artist payments down to approximately 10%.

Of course, the beauty of self publishing is that you can control how your books are sold and how many parties are involved in the production and transportation process. By cutting out a distributor for example, you'll be able to increase the royalties you secure through the sale of each book. Alternatively, you could sell the books yourself at book fairs or at book talks which would remove the need to pay a bookstore to sell your books for you.

The table below illustrates how the percentage of royalties you receive can change depending on how much of the book production and transportation process you undertake yourself. The figures used are averages, and will change slightly depending on where, when and how many of your books are produced and sold at any one time.

| Option | Printers | Distributors | Bookseller | Artist | Percentage of royalties received by author |
|--------|----------|--------------|------------|--------|---------------------------------------------|
| 1 | √ | √ | √ | √ | 10% |
| 2 | √ | √ | √ | | 20% |
| 3 | √ | | √ | √ | 30% |
| 4 | √ | | √ | | 40% |
| 5 | √ | | | √ | 60% |
| 6 | √ | | | | 80% |

'You could sell the books yourself at book fairs or at book talks which would remove the need to pay a bookstore to sell your books for you.'

# Quantities

If you choose to sell copies of your book yourself; perhaps to friends, at book talks, your book launch or at book fairs, then you'll be able to place an order for a set quantity of books to be printed by your chosen printing house, ready for your own distribution.

Lots of self-publishing authors fall into the trap of ordering too many copies of their book to be printed; attracted by the fact that the printing price per book copy tends to drop as the size of the order placed rises. By reducing the printing price per book, authors see that they will increase their profit margin on each book sold. This is true . . . however only if all printed copies are sold. Self-publishing experts therefore strongly recommend that self-publishing authors limit their initial printing orders to 100 copies or less, as it is almost always harder to sell copies of your book than initially thought.

# How to record royalties

It is important to record the royalty payments you receive from your self-published book, as they are classified as income and so must be declared to the tax office on an annual basis. However, there are lots of expenses that you can put forward as tax deductible items, and so these will reduce the amount of tax that you have to pay on any royalties received.

It is therefore important to keep accurate and up-to-date records of the money that you receive through the sale of your book, and of the expenses you incur through the enhancement, advancement or promotion of your book and writing in general.

## What counts as an expense?

Any costs you have incurred through the writing, production, printing, promoting and selling of your book are likely to be counted as an expense. This means that you can offset them against the profits made through your book sales. Examples of deductible expenses include:

- Office supplies.

- Membership fees for any writing groups or associations.

- Postage used for the sending out of material related to your book production or promotion.

- Costs incurred when attending writing conferences (fees, travel, accommodation, etc.).

- Writing-related books.

- Trips taken for research or book promotion purposes.

'It is important to record the royalty payments you receive from your self-published book, as they are classified as income and so must be declared to the tax office.'

- The cost from service suppliers (editors, printers, distributors, etc.).
- Promotional resources (posters, launch party invitations etc.).

## Record keeping

When it comes to reporting your royalties and your expenses, solid record keeping is crucial. It is also relatively easy to do, as long as you do it on a regular basis.

To record your expenses you first need to ensure that you have a receipt for each and every expense you are looking to claim for. Put these receipts into a plastic wallet or into an envelope to keep them safe and secure. It might be easier to use a different wallet or envelope for each month; that way a specific receipt will be easy to locate in the future.

As you gather up each receipt, you need to record the total cost paid out onto a spreadsheet. You should also record when that expense occurred, and what the expense related to. The table below demonstrates how the spreadsheet rows and columns could be laid out:

| Date | Expense type | Amount spent |
|------|--------------|--------------|
| 02.09.2011 | Postage of review copies of books to local press | £13.77 |
| 02.09.2011 | Purchase of printer paper and A4 envelopes for distribution of launch party promotional posters | £21.97 |
| 04.09.2011 | Invoice from caterers for launch party finger buffet | £317.88 |
| 07.09.2011 | Annual writing group membership | £45.00 |
| **Running Total** | | **£398.62** |

Next, you need to record your royalties – any money you receive through the sale of your books. This can either be recorded on a different tab within the same spreadsheet, on a new spreadsheet, or as a separate table on the same spreadsheet page as the expenses table.

Royalty payments should be recorded on your spreadsheet as and when they are received. As with expenses, you need to record; (a) when a payment has been made, (b) where the royalty payment came from, and (c) how much the payment was for.

Each royalty payment received should have some supporting paperwork to demonstrate that the payment has been made. This might be a statement from the self-publishing company that is managing the distribution of your books for you, or, if you are managing the sales process of your book yourself, it might be a copy of the invoice that you send to sellers when they request copies of your book. Ensure you keep a copy of this supporting paperwork, just in case your accounts are ever audited.

'You will also need to declare the expenses you've incurred, as these can act as a tax relief against any tax due.'

# How to declare royalties

Payments received through royalties need to be declared to HM Revenue & Customs, via a self-assessment tax return. If you are employed, you may not automatically receive a self-assessment tax form to complete, but you can request one from HM Revenue & Customs, or ask an accountant to do so on your behalf.

On the tax return there is a section which asks individuals to record any 'other income' – this is anything over and above what you've earned by working. 'Other income' could include; income from savings, income from property, pensions, and miscellaneous income, which includes royalties paid to authors. Here you need to record the money you've received through royalty payments. However you will also need to declare the expenses you've incurred, as these can act as a tax relief against any tax that you are due to pay on your royalties.

# Summing Up

■ The term 'royalties' relates to the money an author receives following the sale of one or more copies of their book. This money is usually a percentage of the book cover price, and will be calculated once book printers, distributors and sellers have all received payment. For self-publishing authors, a royalty payment can be anywhere between 10% and 80% of the book's cover price.

■ Royalty payments must be declared to the tax office on an annual basis, however expenses incurred through the writing, production and promotion of the book can be offset against the tax due on any royalties received. For this reason, it is crucial that writers keep an accurate record of expenses incurred and royalties received.

# Help List

## Useful Organisations

### Amazon

Web: services.amazon.co.uk
Email: Via an online form through the webpage: services.amazon.co.uk/standards/contact-us/

### Author's Licensing and Collecting Society Ltd (ALCS)

The Writer's House, 13 Haydon Street
London EC3 1DB
Web: www.alcs.co.uk
Email: alcs@alcs.co.uk
Tel: 020 7264 5700

### The Independent Publishers' Guild

PO Box 12, Llain, Whitland SA34 0WU
Web: www.ipg.uk.com
Email: info@ipg.uk.com
Tel: 01437 563335

### Nielson

Nielson House, London Road, Headington, Oxford, Oxfordshire, OX3 9RX
Web: www.nielson.com/UK
Email: Via an online form through the webpage: www.nielsen.com/uk/en/contact.html
Tel: 01865 742742

### Society for Editors and Proofreaders (SfEP)

Erico, 93-99 Upper Richmond Road, Putney, London SW15 2TG
Web: www.sfep.org.uk
Tel: 020 8785 5617

### The Society of Authors

84 Drayton Gardens, London SW10 9SB
Web: www.societyofauthors.org
Email: info@societyofauthors.org
Tel: 0207 3736642

### The Society of Indexers

Woodbourne Business Centre, 10 Jessel Street, Sheffield S9 3HY
Web: www.indexers.org.uk
Email: info@indexers.org.uk
Tel: 0114 244 9561

# Book Distributors

## Bertram Books

Web: www.bertrams.com
Email: ros.wesson@bertrams.com
Tel: 0871 803 6600

## Gardners

Web: www.gardners.com
Email: sph@gardners.com
Tel: 01323 521777

# Photography Libraries

www.istockphoto.com
www.gettyimages.co.uk
www.dreamstime.com
www.shutterstock.com

# Marketing Resources

www.venuefinder.com
www.writers-circles.com/circles
www.press-release-writing.com
www.prlong.com (a free press release distribution site)
www.pressbox.co.uk (a free press release distribution site)

# Book List

**Writers' and Artists' Yearbook (annual)**
A & C Black, London
www.writersandartists.co.uk

**The Writer's Handbook (annual)**
By Barry Turner (ed), Macmillan, Hampshire
www.thewritershandbook.co.uk

**Writers' Market (annual)**
By David & Charles, Devon
www.writersmarket.co.uk

## Useful Magazines

**The Self Publishing Magazine**
5 Weir Road
Kibworth Beauchamp
Leicestershire LE8 0LQ
www.selfpublishingmagazine.co.uk

**Writer's Forum**
PO Box 6337, Bournemouth BH1 9EH
Web: www.writers-forum.com

**Writing Magazine & Writers' News**
Warners Group Publications plc, 5th Floor, 31-32 Park Row, Leeds LS1 5JD

# Need - 2 - Know

**Need —2— Know**

## Available Titles Include ...

**Publishing Poetry** The Essential Guide
ISBN 978-1-86144-113-3 £9.99

**Writing Poetry** The Essential Guide
ISBN 978-1-86144-112-6 £9.99

**Writing Non-Fiction Books** The Essential Guide
ISBN 978-1-86144-114-0 £9.99

**Book Proposals** The Essential Guide
ISBN 978-1-86144-118-8 £9.99

**Writing Dialogue** The Essential Guide
ISBN 978-1-86144-119-5 £9.99

**Creating Fictional Characters** The Essential Guide
ISBN 978-1-86144-120-1 £9.99

**Writing Romantic Fiction** The Essential Guide
ISBN 978-1-86144-121-8 £9.99

**Pilates** The Essential Guide
ISBN 978-1-86144-097-6 £9.99

**Surfing** The Essential Guide
ISBN 978-1-86144-106-5 £9.99

**Gardening** A Beginner's Guide
ISBN 978-1-86144-100-3 £9.99

**Going Green** The Essential Guide
ISBN 978-1-86144-089-1 £9.99

**Food for Health** The Essential Guide
ISBN 978-1-86144-095-2 £9.99

**Vegan Cookbook** The Essential Guide
ISBN 978-1-86144-123-2 £9.99

**Walking** A Beginner's Guide
ISBN 978-1-86144-101-0 £9.99

View the full range at **www.need2knowbooks.co.uk**. To order our titles call **01733 898103**, email **sales@n2kbooks.com** or visit the website. Selected ebooks available online.

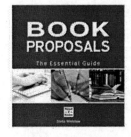

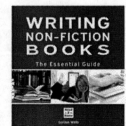

**Need - 2 - Know**, Remus House, Coltsfoot Drive, Peterborough, PE2 9BF